Lorain Roberson (signature)

WHAT COLOR WAS JESUS?

By: William Mosley

African American Images
Chicago, Illinois

PHOTO CREDITS

Interpress Publication	pp. x, 19
Vie De Jesus Mafa	p. 3
Jon Lockhard	p. 5
Saint Sebina	p. 16
Joseph Evans	p. 38
Fernando Arizti	p. 58

Cover Illustration by Cornell Barnes
Photography by William Hall

First Edition

Seventh Printing

Copyright © 1987 by William Mosley

TABLE OF CONTENTS

DEDICATION

This work is dedicated to my aunt, Helen Thomas.

ACKNOWLEDGEMENTS

Special thanks is given to Yemi Toure, Rita Kunjufu, and Mary Lewis for their tremendous editorial assistance. I want to especially thank my editor, Jawanza Kunjufu who coordinated this entire project.
God bless all of you!

INTRODUCTION

And ye shall know the truth and the truth shall make you free...

When he (Joseph) arose, he took the young child (Jesus) and his mother by night, and departed unto Egypt: And was there until the death of Herod: that it might be fulfilled which was spoken of the Lord by the prophet, saying, Out of Egypt have I called my son. Matthew 2:14-5

At a meeting of the Los Angeles A.M.E. Ministerial Alliance, one of my colleagues gave a tremendous presentation on Black Liberation Theology. He shared with us the ideas of J. Deotis Roberts, Archie Smith, James Cone, Henry Mitchell and others. He went on to show that a Black Church without a Black Theology is doing a great disservice to its members and to its community.

The discussion period was informative and intense. One of the comments, however, was particularly powerful. The Rev. Charles Brooks of Walker Temple A.M.E. Church pointed out that he knew of a number of Black pastors who talked supportively about the white Jesus, in their churches. He went on to say that he strongly believed that if Black Theology is to take its rightful position in local congregations, it must address the issue of white religious symbols being used in the Black church. It must address the issue of the white Christ.

To confront the issue and symbol of the white Christ is to confront the issue of how Christianity has been used to perpetuate imperialism, colonialism and racism. It is a struggle to free Christianity from its European-American imposed definition of Whitey-ianity, a definition that has been forced upon the Black, Brown and Yellow people of this world in an attempt to maintain the cultural, political and economic power of white supremacy.

For years, seminaries and churches, scholars and clergy have attempted to avoid the issue of the African presence in the Bible. This scholarly silence continued when it came to the African contribution to the development and growth of the Christian church. This silence was rooted in the need to maintain the religious foundation of white supremacy.

What Color was Jesus seeks to deliver us from the cultural and religious symbols of white supremacy. *What Color was Jesus* seeks to break the intellectual and spiritual chains of religious imperialism. *What Color was Jesus* seeks to expose the theological cover up that has attempted to hide the liberating power of the gospel of Jesus Christ. Praise the Lord for *What Color was Jesus!*

In *What Color was Jesus*, William Mosley has made a tremendous contribution to the Black church, Black liberation theology and all people who are committed to truth. In a comprehensive, inter-disciplinary study Brother Mosley has looked at the problem of the color of Jesus biblically, theologically, historically and psychologically. Praise the Lord for *What Color was Jesus!*

The publishing of this book by African American Images deserves high commendation and community support. This book should be required reading for all Black pastors, seminarians and believers. Whether the individual reader will agree with Brother Mosley's conclusions or not; the fact is, this is a thought provoking, groundbreaking, courageous publication.

Finally, I'll never forget the first time Minister Louis Farrakhan of the Nation of Islam came and spoke at Ward in 1981. The city and many of my colleagues were shocked that a Christian pastor would allow a Muslim to preach from the pulpit at the 11 o'clock hour. It was a beautiful service. The minister spoke with great power and wisdom.

The most moving moment of the service for me came when the minister quoted Revelation 1:14-15 and shared with the congregation that the Jesus that we serve and worship was Black just like us. The congregation's response was electric. I looked down to see the reaction of the mothers of the church (the Stewardesses). There, in their white uniforms, they stood applauding and as I looked closely at the oldest and most conservative I saw a tear of joy fall down her cheek.

Praise God for *What Color was Jesus!* And all the people said, Amen.

Frank M. Reid, III
Pastor
Ward A.M.E. Church
Los Angeles

INTRODUCTION

Charles Finch and Charles Copher wrote articles and presented papers for the *Nile Valley Civilizations Conference* (1984) which discussed the "Kemetic Concept of Christianity" and "Egypt and Ethiopia in the Old Testament." These studies added to the already burgeoning field of the African origins of Judaism and Christianity. Copher had been the most published scholar in this area with several of his articles having appeared across the years in the *Journal of the Interdenominational Theological Center* (Atlanta, Georgia).

As one of the "pillars" of African American scholarship based at Morehouse in Atlanta, Dr. Copher has consistently shown through linguistics and word studies that the Bible has its roots on African soil and that the people portrayed on its pages are African people! Arthur Koestler, a Scottish scholar, picks up where Copher leaves off and demonstrates in his *The Thirteenth Tribe* that there were no European Jews until the 7th Century A.D. Everybody in the Old Testament was African (Black) and no white person appears until mention is made of the Roman occupation.

With Copher and Koestler laying such an airtight framework and foundation, it can only follow, then, that a baby boy, born to an African carpenter and his African wife, is both by the laws of logic and genetics bound to be an African baby (with "feet like unto fine brass as if burned in a furnace," and with hair "like wool").

Such is the scandal of the gospel: that God would enter into history (the Incarnation) at a particular time, in a particular place, and as a member of a particular race.

God cannot become a human without being some kind of human! For God to leave the category of the Eternal and enter into a time-space continuum means that God has to become Asian if entering time through the continent and the people of Asia. God has to become European if entering time through the continent and the people of Europe; and God has to become African if entering time through the continent and the people of Africa. God cannot become a "universal" human being. God has to become some specific human being if God is to become Incarnate.

Such a miracle is what the Bible records; but the fact that that miracle means that the Incarnate God, Jesus, is African and not Michelangelo's model has been a doubly disturbing fact for most white people brainwashed (or "miseducated" to use Carter G. Woodson's term) in the post-Enlightment West! The historical facts do not lie. The biblical facts do not lie; but what has happened is that since the Renaissance when Italian models began to be used to portray Biblical themes and the movable printing press began to proliferate those Images of a "white" Jesus, a "white" Abraham and "white" North Africans, most persons began to see painted images which subtly lied and still lie; and began to believe the lies they saw rather than the truth they read.

In Cornell West's *Prophesy Deliverance!*, Dr. West traces the "genealogy of Racism" back through this modern period which we call the Renaissance, and he demonstrates that because of this racism, European standards of beauty became everybody's standard of beauty, that Europe set the norm; and that everything non-European became ugly and abnormal. Things African are about as far from being European as one can get; so the implication that everything African was to be rejected — even the truth recorded in Holy Writ!

It has taken scholars like Leo Hansberry and Chancellor Williams years to undo what the racist writing of European scholars and historians have done. Hansberry and Williams have painstakingly and patiently demonstrated that what has passed itself off as African and African American history (written by whites) has been nothing more than intentional distortions and outright lies. Joining these two giants is an impressive array of brilliant men and women whose studies have sought to correct the distortions and destroy the lies perpetuated by racist minds.

These men and women include Cheikh Ante Diop, Ivan Van Sertima, Lorenzo Dow Turner, John Jackson, Margaret Lee, J.A. Rogers, Jacob Carruthers, Gloria Smitherman, Yosef Ben-Jochannan, Jawanza Kunjufu, Iva Carruthers, Maulana Karenga, Edward Sims, Ayanna Karanja, Sokoni Karanja, Frank Snowden, Joseph Harris and John Henrik Clarke. They join with Bruce Williams, John Pappademos, Beatrice Lumpkin, Na'im Akbar, Asa Hilliard, Frances Holliday and Runoko Rashidi whose combined works are devastating to the distortions disseminated by Eurocentric Miseducation.

Joining this array of brilliant scholars now is William Mosley whose work contributes to this all important area of scholarship. I celebrate Mosley's efforts because of the psychological damage done to African American children who grew up wanting to be like a white Jesus! I celebrate his efforts because they are an outright attack on the disease of racism and color consciousness which seeks to take Egypt out of Africa and put it in a nebulous "Middle East" — a disease which seeks to make biblical Egyptians white or light skinned, and a disease which seeks to move Palestine (where Jesus walked) off the continent of Africa.

I encourage those who pursue honest scholarship and who have no other agenda other than truth; and I look forward to more scholars picking up the gauntlet which Mosley has thrown down, using, perhaps, the works of Albert Cleage, Charles Finch, Charles Copher and Arthur Koestler to further clarify this crucial issue and all the implications it has both psychologically and theologically.

Rev. Dr. Jeremiah A. Wright, Jr.
Pastor
Trinity United Church of Christ
Chicago

You are the most blessed of all women, and blessed is the child you will bear.

Chapter One

The Messiah was Black

From humanity's beginning to the present—and, surely, on into the foreseeable future—one characteristic has remained with Black people: We are a spiritual people.

We have been kings, and we have been slaves; we have been the rulers of the world, and we have been the wretched of the Earth; we have been the subjects of history, and we have been the objects of history; we have been entombed in pyramids, and we have lived in projects.

But the one everlasting idea that has remained with us, sustained us, and in fact has been a central part of our being, is our belief in the spiritual, our belief in that which cannot be perceived solely by the five senses.

For most Black people in the U.S. and for many Black people around the world, this spirituality manifests itself in a belief in God and in Jesus Christ.

Jesus Christ joins with God Himself in the Holy Pantheon of the Christian world. He is the Son in the Holy Trinity of the Father, the Son and the Holy Ghost. His coming to Earth is so important that in the Western World time itself is measured by His birth.

Jesus Christ walked the Earth nearly 2,000 years ago and brought a message of justice, love, hope, and salvation to the world. He is the most powerful earthly manifestation of Christianity.

Jesus Christ can be seen. Ask anyone to think of Jesus, and the image of a man will come to mind.

But alas, even the image of Jesus Christ is not exempt from the

1

impact of White racism. What color was Jesus? What was the length and color and texture of His hair? What color were His eyes? What was the shape of His nose and the size of His lips?

Indeed, is it possible to hold an image of Jesus in our minds and not think of His race? And what race do we think He is? Do we, in fact, think of Jesus as White?

Look inside any Black church today for the image of Jesus. In many instances, you will find that He is depicted as White in pictures in the Sunday School lessons. In the hot summer, the ushers pass out fans with a drawing of a white Jesus, and as the sun shines through stained glass windows, the image of a white Jesus is cast across the congregation.

Indeed, one of the most amazing elements of White racism is that our vision of Jesus, this Prince of Peace who at this very moment sits at the right hand of God Himself—our vision even of Jesus Christ Himself has been distorted by racism.

The distorted notion that Jesus was White can be traced back to its origins. But then, one must confront the next question:

What color was Jesus? The question is a bold one. Anybody who asks it can expect a barrage of attacks so intense one would mistakenly think it was coming from above. There were no photographs taken of our Lord and Savior, so we can only make inferences.

But the best way to respond to your attackers is to calmly open your Bible—or preferably theirs.

A sensitive review of Scriptures will lead to clearer understanding. Ezekiel, Daniel and Revelations depict God Himself or the Son of God with hair like "wool," and with bodily parts the color of "brass" and "amber" (cf. Ezekiel 1:27 & 8:2; Daniel 7:9; Revelation 1:14-15).

Further, look at Jesus' family tree. Reverend Walter Arthur McCray points to several biblical references and explains: "That Jesus Christ had Black ancestors, that is, people of Hamitic origin in His family line, can be demonstrated quite simply.

"The genealogical information about Jesus Christ is provided us in two Gospels: Matthew 1:1-16 and Luke 3:23-38. These genealogical tables are reliable, providing detailed information about the Lord's ancestry.

There are basically two views held by biblical scholars concerning these genealogical tables. One view has it that the genealogical table in Matthew gives Joseph's family tree and that the

A virgin will become pregnant and have a son, and he will be called Jesus.

one in Luke gives Mary's family tree. The other view has it that the genealogical information in both Gospels gives only Joseph's line. As such, Matthew's information provides the line of official succession to the Davidic throne, and Luke's information gives details of the actual physical ancestors of Joseph back to David.

Whichever view of the Gospel's information is accepted, it will become evident that both genealogical tables have a significant bearing on the fact that Christ Jesus had Black (African), that is, Hamitic ancestors. Before we give the simple details, let us first establish the ancient family tree of Black people as recorded in the Scriptures.

It is acceptable by both biblical and non-biblical scholars that Hamitic peoples are the ancestors and originators of African peoples all over the earth. Who then was Ham, the father of Hamitic peoples?

From the holy and historical record of Genesis (5:32; 9:18; 10:1, 6-20, 32) we learn that Ham was one of the three sons of Noah who survived the flood which destroyed all the earth. Only eight people remained following the flood. These eight people were Noah and his wife, Noah's three sons, Shem, Ham, and Japheth, each with his own wife. It was from these eight persons the the world was repopulated following the flood.

3

Concerning Ham, he became the father of Cush, Egypt, Put and Canaan—all Black sons of their Black father. These sons became nations in their own right, giving birth to other peoples.

At this point we are now in a position to appreciate the Black ancestry of Christ. This information is anchored in the genealogical table of Matthew, and to our surprise it concerns no less than three of the four women who are noted as being ancestors of the Lord!

The first woman is mentioned in Matthew 1:3 (Revised Standard Version) and is named Tamar. The story of Tamar can be found in Genesis 38. Tamar was known to be a Canaanite woman by virtue of where she dwelt, in a city called Timnath. Timnath was in the vicinity of Adullam, a known Canaanite town (cf. 38:1, 2, 6, 11, 13). Tamar became an ancestor of Christ Jesus through a child she mothered by her own father-in-law Judah. The child's name was Perez (Matthew 1:3).

The second woman is mentioned in Matthew 1:5 and is named Rahab. The story of Rahab is found in Joshua 2:1-21 and 6:17-25. Rahab was known to be a Canaanite, and inhabitant of the city of Jericho. She was the prostitute who helped the two Israelite spies when they surveyed the land of Canaan. As a result of her actions of faith, the lives of Rahab and her household were spared during the Israelite conquest of Jericho (cf. Hebrews 11:31; James 2:25). It was an ancestor of Christ Jesus named Boaz who was in fact the son of Rahab the Canaanite (Matthew 1:5).

The third woman who was a Black ancestor of Christ Jesus is mentioned in Matthew 1:6 as the 'wife of Uriah,' Bathsheba by name. The story of Bathsheba is recorded in 2 Samuel 11. Most know the story of David and Bathsheba. What is often overlooked is the fact that Bathsheba was married to Uriah the Hittite. It is widely known and accepted that the Hittites were a Hamitic people. They descended from Heth, a son of Canaan (Genesis 10:15; 23:10). If in fact Bathsheba shared the same ethnic origin as her husband (a not improbable assumption), then the child born to her and David, Solomon by name, did indeed have Black ancestry in his veins. Solomon was an ancestor of Christ Jesus (Matthew 1:6).

Immediately the objection may be raised: But Joseph, whose genealogy is recorded in Matthew's Gospel, had nothing to do with the birth of Jesus, for Jesus was miraculously conceived and born to a woman who was a virgin. Joseph's seed had nothing to do with the humanity of Jesus. Thus, any reference to Black African blood in the genealogical line of Jesus through Joseph is invalid!

Such an objection would be devastating to our argument, save for one bit of enlightening information. It is virtually without disagreement among biblical scholars that Mary as well as Joseph was 'of the house of David' (Luke 1:27, RSV; cf. Luke 2:4). This blood relation of Mary to her forefather King David is corroborated by other Scripture (see Luke 1:32, 69; Matthew 9:27; 15:22; 20:30, 31; Mark 10:47, 48).

That Mary, as the woman who physically mothered Christ, was of David's line is foreshadowed in the prophecies that the promised Messiah was to be the very offspring of David as well as successor to the Davidic throne (cf. 2 Samuel 7:12ff.; 1 Kings 8:25-26; Isaiah 7:2, 13-14; 9:7; Jeremiah 23:5; 33:15, 17, 22, 25-26; John 7:42; Mark 11:10). Indeed, according to His own testimony, Christ Jesus Himself is both 'the root and the offspring of David' (Revelation 22:15)."

When I was a child, I spoke as a child,
but when I became a man, I put
away childish ways.

5

"Now inasmuch as the references to women of Hamitic descent impact upon the 'house of David,' Jesus' lineage is so affected by virtue of Mary His mother. This is true in both the cases of Tamar and Rahab, for they preceded David and his house. Further, it may not be unreasonable to assume that Mary's bloodline may also have been influenced through Solomon, the son of Bathsheba and David. The fact that Luke's Gospel carries a heightened emphasis on the very physical descent of Christ gives an added strength to this argument.

"So here we have it, Tamar, Rahab, and Bathsheba—each of Hamitic descent, each a lineal ancestor of Christ Jesus according to reliable genealogical information of Matthew's and Luke's Gospels. Ontologically speaking, then, Jesus is Black, for 'Black' blood ran in His human veins.

"Such truth concerning the racial identity of Jesus is liberating to many of us, despite the fact that a racial relationship to Christ may serve for Black people only as a cordial invitation to Christ. For each person, of whatever racial origin, must personally come to the Lord for salvation, regardless of a kinship relationship to Christ Jesus."[1]

This led Bishop Alfred G. Dunston Jr. to conclude in *The Black Man in the Old Testament and its World*:

"When all the available facts are examined, we know beyond doubt that the black presence was one of the dominant elements in the original native Egyptian population, and furthermore we know that Cushite (Ethiopian) [people] formed a large part in the Egyptian population of Israel's day. In truth, it must be admitted that Moses perhaps led more black people out of Egypt than those of other colors."[2]

McCray traces the use of biblical terms that predated the word 'Black': "The student of Scripture cannot identify Black people in the Bible by the terms 'Negro,' 'Black,' 'Afro-American,' 'African-American,' or 'African.' The person who traces this line of thought will search in vain. . . . The basic term which is used to identify [Africans] in the Bible is the word 'Ethiopian' or 'Cush,' or one of their derivatives." These include Kush, Kushite, Cushi, Cushite, Ethiopian, Egypt, Seba, Havilah, Sabtah, Raama and Sheba. Kush is the name given by Egypt to her southern neighbor. Ethiopian is a Greek term; they applied it to the lands south of Egypt. It means "burnt-faced."[3]

It is the nature of Bible translations to make the word of God clear to the intended readers. Translators read the original languages in which the Bible was written (Hebrew in the Old Testament and Greek in the New Testament) and translate these languages into the language of the reader. This process of translation allows the translator's opinion (interpretations) to ease into the translation whether for good or bad. King James of England in the seventeenth century was familiar with Africans but refused to clarify the terms. The term "Ethiopian" did not image a Black person to the English reading White mind, but it imaged a white person in "blackish color" due to the hair texture, skin color, Arabian heritage, and geographical location of the modern Ethiopian people. Why? Simply because the King James translator refused to identify Africans whom they held as slaves with the Africans written about in the Bible.

Let us look to biblical history to piece the puzzle together. If we acknowledge the archaeological findings that earliest man originated in northeastern Africa, then what is written the Bible as it pertains to the creation of man and the Garden of Eden is confirmed. In establishing exactly where the Garden was, the book of Genesis cites the four rivers—Pishon, Gihon (in the land of Kush-Ethiopia), Tigris and Euphrates—which run through Syria and Iraq. These two countries were also connected to Africa before the construction of the Suez Canal.[4]

So if the original Hebrews were a non-White stock, we may conclude that the original Israelites were considerably more Black at the time of the Exodus than present-day Israelis.

Furthermore, the historical record says that ancient Israel, Egypt, and Ethiopia were not only close geographically, but were also close socially, culturally, economically, and politically.

Both sacred and secular writing describe the presence of Ethiopian peoples in Egypt and Israel from the Exodus to the birth of Jesus of Nazareth. Also, the Ethiopian peoples of ancient times were comparable to present-day Sudanese people; that is, they were Africans that anthropologists would call the Negroid type: full-blooded, black-skinned, broad-featured.

In short, if there was an assimilation of Black peoples among the Israelites, and there was; and if Jesus was an Israelite, and He was; then Jesus might very well have inherited genes from Ethiopian ancestors, which would have made Him Black.

Footnotes

1. Reverend Walter Arthur McCray, "The Black Lineage of Christ Jesus" (Chicago: Black Light Fellowship, 1987), n.p., used by permission.

2. Alfred G. Dunston, Jr., *The Black Man in the Old Testament and its World* (Philadelphia: Dorrance and Company, 1974), p. 72.

3. Reverend Walter Arthur McCray, *The Black Presence in The Bible* (Chicago: Black Light Fellowship, 1985), p. 7.

4. Ben Ammi, *God the Black Man and Truth* (Chicago: Communicators Press, 1982), p. 7.

Chapter Two

How Christ Became White

Color Prejudice in the Early Christian Church

Distinct notions of European Christianity, culture, and consciousness emerged gradually and simultaneously during the first century after Christ. Preceding that development, the only large cohesive European community in existence was that which encompassed the Mediterranean world under Greco-Roman rule.

Not only Christianity but its central figure, Jesus Christ, provided a previously unintegrated community of developing nations the supreme ideal symbol around which they would then begin to merge into a viable cultural force with a unified sense of racial self-consciousness.

"Christianity," says Joel Kovel, author of *White Racism: A Psycho history:*

". . .spread over the west and created a community out of what had been barbarian splinters. It did this through the power of a concrete institution, the Catholic Church. It was the Church's immediate influence that held aloft the subliminatory ideal of Christ and, through that ideal, gave Europeans a scaffold of identification with which to bind themselves into a unified civilization."[1]

With the development of this European consciousness, including its newfound, unified cultural identity in Christ, came the practice of creating and enshrining sacred figures to conform with physical European models and standards. The physical features of Jesus, in time, became typically Aryan, often complete

9

with blue eyes, long straight hair, thin lips and a keen sharp nose, and his color, progressively, became a perfect reflection of pale white European skin.

How did Whites come to this? Such pervasive and perverse ideas did not develop out of thin air. There was a racist ground in which this bad seed was planted.

In *Nature Knows No Color Line*, the Black historian J.A. Rogers, who was also a journalist and a prodigious writer, documents the existence of racial prejudice before the time of Christ and European Christianity. According to Rogers, the earliest evidence of color prejudice is found in the Vedic scriptures . . .in India of some five thousand years ago when Aryas, or Aryans, invaded the valley of the Indus and found there a black people— the Dasysus, or Dasyus."[2]

Even in ancient dynastic Egypt, during those brief periods when lighter-complexioned groups dominated the land, evidence exists to show that the darker-complexioned Kushites were sometimes called "the evil race."

In an article entitled "A Vanishing Problem," Jacques Duchesne-Guillemin tells of the symbolic use of black, white, and red colors as an ancient European tradition:

". . .if the distinction between the Negro, the whitebearded old man, and the red-cheeked youth succeeded in imposing itself and becoming permanent, is it not partly because it fitted into a pattern of colors which was already in existence in European folklore and perhaps even in the Indo-European ideology, or earlier yet?"[3]

But Frank M. Snowden, in *Blacks in Antiquity: Ethiopians in the Greco-Roman Experience*, strongly contends that distinct pre-Christian color awareness in Greek and Roman antiquity did not present a serious bar to relations between Blacks and Whites. He does admit, however, that: "There was a belief in certain circles that the color of the Ethiopians' skin was ominous, related no doubt to the association of the color black with death, the underworld, and evil."[4]

The Romans were instrumental in spreading Christianity throughout the Western world as it was then known. Notwithstanding Asian, African, and Eastern European influence, it was the Western powers, with Rome at the center, that opened the way for racial and color prejudices to infiltrate the organized Christian Church and cast the die that would eventually alter

10

and corrupt the symbolic perceptions of the White world.

With this foundation—and because of sharp skin color differences, especially between Caucasoid peoples (Europeans) and Negroid peoples (Africans)—fear and antagonism by Europeans toward Africans were inevitable.

Snowden claims that the early Christian attitude toward Blacks followed a view that was patterned after the Greco-Roman tendency to stress only the contrast between Blacks and Whites and not to point out a notion of equality.

Snowden says that one of the earliest instances of special emphasis being placed on Ethiopian features, e.g., "flat nose, thick lips, wooly hair," is recorded in Xenophanes of Colophon in mid-fifth century B.C.[5]

In support of the allegation that Babylonian rabbis were the first in the West to suggest qualitative differences between Blacks and Whites, Rogers quotes the French anthropologist Topinard:

"In the first century when Christianity was beginning to seat itself in Rome the doctrine of a separate creation for whites and blacks was defended by the Babylonian rabbis and later by Emperor Julian."[6]

The infamous mythological dogma that black skin is the consequence of Noah's curse on his son Ham was introduced at about the same time. According to early interpretations of Genesis 10, blackness of skin was visited on Ham's descendants through his son Canaan.

Ham allegedly sinned against Noah, and therefore God, with the consequence that the "curse" of blackness of skin became associated with sin.

Roger Bastide, author of an important article entitled "Color, Racism, and Christianity," underscores this idea by saying, "Over and above any historical and economic factors, the roots of segregation are to be found in the idea of contagiousness of sin through color."[7]

Hence, the anathema of sin passed over into the anathema of race through prejudicial color symbolism.

In *Race: The History of an Idea in America*, Thomas F. Gossett refers to the different interpretations of the Noah incident:

"There is some confusion in the account in Genesis because it is not clear whether the curse was to be visited upon Ham or upon Canaan, the son of Ham. Modern critics usually regard the story as having been told originally of Canaan, Ham being a later insertion. Nothing is said in Genesis about the descendants of either Ham or Canaan being Negroes. This idea is not found until the oral traditions of the Jews were collected in the Babylonian Talmud from the second century to the sixth century A.D. In this source, the descendants of Ham are said to be cursed by being black. In the Talmud there are several contradictory legends concerning Ham—one that God forbade anyone to have sexual relations while on the Ark and Ham disobeyed this command. Another story is that Ham was cursed with blackness because he resented the fact that his father desired to have a fourth son. To prevent the birth of a rival heir, Ham is said to have castrated his father. Elsewhere in the Talmud, Ham's descendants are depicted as being led into captivity with their buttocks uncovered as a sign of their degradation."[8]

In the Babylonian Talmud, Tractate, *Sanhedrin 108b*, the following account is given:

"Our Rabbis taught: three copulated in the ark, and they were all punished—the dog, the raven and Ham. The dog was doomed to be tied, the raven expectorates (his seed into his mate's mouth) and Ham was smitten in his skin."[9]

Rabbis argue here that blackness is due to copulation in the ark as opposed to the Christian view that it resulted from looking at or disrespecting Noah's nakedness.

The Impetus for a White Jesus

Whereas color prejudice did exist early in the history of the Christian Church, color connotation, equating black with sin and white with purity, existed previously. Yet, it was not until the fifteenth century, when the Atlantic slave trade began under the Portuguese, that racism began to emerge in its most deadly theological, philosophical, and scientific forms.

"Not long after the first slaves were taken from Africa by Europeans, Pope Julius II in 1505 commissioned the painting of certain biblical works from artist Michaelangelo and in doing... so initiated the concept of God as being White. Included in the painting is the portrait of Mary, mother of Jesus, whose prominent Black features were distorted to resemble a Florentine Italian woman. Likewise, in the Michelangelo paintings, the images of the Christ child, the three wise men, the Lord's Supper and the Resurrection, were changed until no trace of their original Blackness remained. Not only were these images changed, but entire nations, peoples and empires were changed, like the ancient Egyptians, the Israelites, Babylonians, Persians, and Chinese. The features came to resemble those of caucasian ancestry. Thus, we have Michelangelo, Leonardo de Vinci and others to thank for artistically changing the face of the world from Black to White."[10]

The logic of Western color connotation and its concurrent symbolism demanded, of course, the rescue of Jesus Christ from every vestige and suggestion of Blackness. Thus White theology evolved into a system of religious thought reflective of its anti-Black, pro-European biases and origins.

Logically, the only color concept that fit this theology was Whiteness, since to have Jesus participate in Blackness would be to place Him under a divinely ordained curse. Another contradiction would have been the belief that Jesus was not White yet White people were morally, spiritually, intellectually and otherwise superior to non-Whites.

In Bastide's words: "...it was necessary that this man, the incarnation of God, be as far removed as possible from every thing that could suggest darkness, or blackness, even indirectly."[11]

This Christian tradition has other important aspects. According to Eric Neuman in *Depth Psychology and a New Ethic,* Judeo-Christian ideals—rationality, temperance, order, discipline, moral consciousness—represent Western man's ideals.[12] These values are centered deep in the psyche and constitute a moral value system.

Some psychologists say, however, that there is also a negative part of the Western experience which is centered just as deep in the psyche. Some call this part of the psyche dark, mysterious, irrational, deceitful and immoral. The term "shadow" symbolizes this complex of passions, hostilities, aggressions, ambiguities, incivilities, and conflicts.

With all these secret corruptions inexorably afflicting the Western mind, inevitably, the concept of Blackness became synonym and symbol for these negative ideas.

With these internal psychic contradictions, there developed a need for a scapegoat. Soon, the conflict between light and dark, good and evil, purity and impurity, holiness and sin, integrity and corruption, white and black, ceased to be solely internal and

13

invisible: instead, it became a struggle with external and visible forces.

How did it play itself out? Moral compulsions to wipe out these despised anti-Christian forces were expressed—in war, racism, genocide, imperialism—against darker-skinned peoples.

And since these peoples represented 180-degree deviations from the Nordic and Anglo-Saxon norm, they became the primary targets of these "shadow compulsions." Neumann concludes:

"Inside a nation, the aliens who provide the objects for this projection are the minorities; if these are of a different racial or ethnological complexion or, better still, of a different color, their suitability for this purpose is particularly obvious. This psychological problem of the minorities is to be found with religious, national, racial and social variations; it is, however, symptomatic, in every case, of a split in the structure of the collective psyche. The role of the alien, which was played in former times by prisoner of war or shipwrecked mariners, is now being played by the Chinese, the Negroes, and the Jews. The same principle governs the treatment of religious minorities in all religions; and the Fascist plays the same part in a Communist society as the Communist in a Fascist society."[13]

These "shadow compulsions" reached their epitome in the atrocious expression of White racism by which Black people in the United States were and are victimized.

It is obvious that no Black Jesus could reign over this world: He had to be White. So now the circle was complete. Since peoples with light skin "obviously" had been chosen over the "pagan" children of darkness to spread the "light" of the Christian gospel, the practice of slavery, oppression, and colonialism could then be rationalized on ethical and theological grounds.

And the proof of Europeans' "divine election" to Whiteness was to be found in economic prosperity; evidence of non-Europeans' damnation was found in economic poverty. Whatever conditions enabled Whites to justify the colonization and enslavement of Blacks, it is certain that economic interests played a major role.

Concomitantly, religious and philosophical conditioning reinforced this economic dominance and exploitation. What better justification could White exploiters hope for than an indictment of men with Black skin handed down from Deity? For Black people, the reversal of the Apostle Paul's words in Romans 8:31

would make them nonetheless true: "If God be against us, then who can be for us?"

Footnotes

1. Joel Kovel, *White Racism: A Psychohistory* (New York: Random House, Inc., 1970), pp. 145-6.
2. J. A. Rogers, *Nature Knows No Color Line* (New York: Helga M. Rogers), p. 7.
3. Jacques Duchesne-Guillemin, *Myths and Symbols: Studies in Honor of Mircea Eliade*, eds., Joseph M. Kitagawa and Charles H. Long (Chicago and London: University of Chicago Press, 1969), p. 277.
4. Frank M. Snowden, *Blacks in Antiquity: Ethiopians in the Greco-Roman Experience*, (Cambridge, Mass.: Harvard University Press, 1970), p. 179.
5. Snowden, p. 171.
6. Rogers, *Nature*, etc., p. 10.
7. Roger Bastide, *"Color, Racism, and Christianity," Color and Race*, ed., John Hope Franklin (Boston: Beacon Press, 1969), p. 42.
8. Thomas F. Gossett, *Race: The History of an Idea in America* (New York: Schocken Books, 1968), p. 5.
9. Babylonian Talmud, Tractate, *Sanhedrin 108b*.
10. Ammi, p. 10.
11. Bastide, p. 32.
12. Eric Neumann, *Depth Psychology and a New Ethic* (New York: Harper and Row Publishers, 1969, 1973), pp. 138-9.
13. Ibid., p. 52.

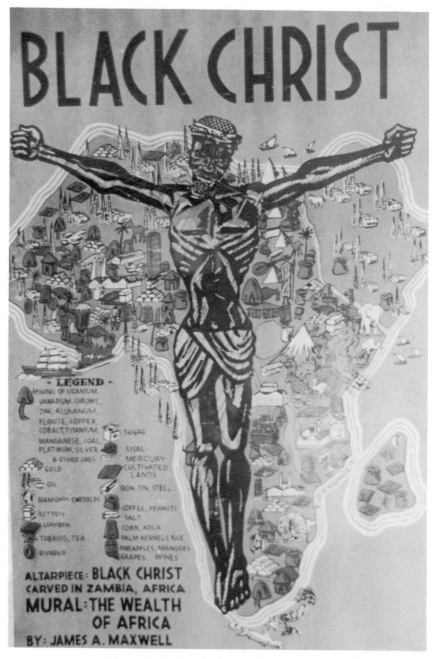

The belief in one God started in Africa.

Chapter Three

World Perspectives on the Black Messiah

African Perspectives

Since Africa is the motherland of humanity, it is to be expected that Christ would also be at home there. For many of the peoples of Africa, black is a sacred color, so God in an African form would only be natural.

In "Bantu Messiah and White Christ," Bengt Sundkler, a Swedish scholar and missionary, echoes these African sentiments:

"Second Corinthians 4:4 and Colossians 1:15 speak of Christ as the image or ikon of God. The important question for the African is this: When God turns to the Whites, he obviously used the image (ikon, persona) which they call the White Christ; but when he turns to us, the Bantu, what form and what image does he use in order to make himself known to us?"[1]

Sundkler's visit to Johannesburg, South Africa, enabled him to see and hear "how mission churches and separatist groups struggled with the problem of the White Christ."[2] It is a struggle that exists all over the continent of Africa, taking on many forms.

Donna Beatrice is the European name of a Kongolese girl, Kimpa Vita, whose religious career took the shape of that of a prophet. In *Kimbangu: An African Prophet and His Church*, Marie-Louise Martin says Vita influenced a large following, teaching that "Christ was born as an African in Sao Salvador and that his apostles were blacks."[3] She and her followers wanted to know how could "the Christ of the exploiting European, help the suffering Africans who were longing for liberation?"[4]

Similarly, A. E. Beyioku started the Orunmia movement in Nigeria in 1943. This movement began among the Yoruba people in the Lagos area, teaching that Jesus Christ was African and making such proclamations as:

"Let the image of God be African. Let the angels be African as well and paint the devil any color you choose, but never the color of the Negro race. Have faith in the cult of Orunmia and you shall be saved!"[5]

Color means one thing in Europe; it means quite another in Africa. Especially on the level of color as symbol, the connotations of color and how color is interpreted, African cultural forms are bound to be antagonistic to European ones.

An example of this difference is found in Xenophanes who, according to author Frank M. Snowden: "...stated that the Ethiopians represented their gods as black-faced and flat-nosed, whereas the Thracians [an Indo-European people] showed their gods to be blue-eyed and red haired."[6]

Ethiopian representations of biblical personages almost invariably carry the colors and features of Ethiopians.

In contemporary Africa, this tendency remains; the correlation between art and religion does not go unacknowledged.

Arna Lehmann expresses this in his *Christian Art in Africa and Asia*. This struggle for personal, ethnic and religious identity against oppression in the area of color symbolism is articulated in the "...extremely vocal insistence on a black Christ in the Separatist churches, where the aversion to everything Western is especially pronounced. There the foolish virgins have slyly become white and the wise virgins black."[7]

Concerning a twentieth century African wood carving titled *Christ with the Crown of Thorns*, Lehmann perceptively comements:

"It is the face of Christ crowned with thorns, a black Christ carved on a book end out of some dark wood that has been sanded and mellowed to a soft sheen. You ache to run your fingers down the bridge of the nose and the great, full lips; to trace the cool plane of the cheeks where the swirl of the grain has become the track of dried tears, the scar running down into one eyebrow where the wood was cracked. There is no way of saying all that shines out of such a face other than the way the wood has said it. Compassion, beauty, sorrow, majesty, love—as words they are so freighted with meaning that they finally founder. The wood is mute. What it tells us is simply all there is to tell about what it means to be black, what it means to be a man, what it means to be God."[8]

The Shrine of the Black Madonna and The Prince of Peace.

The Black Messiah and Madonna in Eurasia

The ancient Egyptian dieties Isis and Orisis were worshipped throughout much of Asia and Europe before and after the coming of Christianity. The influence of these dieties is sometimes seen as the reason there are so many ancient images of a Black Madonna and Child. J. A. Rogers notes: "God. . .on all the continents [was] black. Research has yielded an impressive amount of material on the subject. Moreover, the word, Christ, comes from Indian, Krishna or Chrishna, which means 'The Black One.'[9]

Rogers further claims that the god Osiris of ancient Egypt, the Krishnas of India; the buddhas of India, China and Japan; Laotsze of China; the Fuhi of China; the Sommonacom of Siam; the Xaha of Japan; the ancient Druid gods; and the gods of Greece were Black. These Grecian gods included Jupiter, Baccus, Hercules, Apollo and Ammon; and the goddesses Isis, Venus, Hecati, Juno, Metis, Ceres and Cybele; the latter were all worshipped in Rome.[10]

19

J. A. Rogers then quotes Godfrey Higgins' Anacalypsis:

"In all the Romish countries of Europe, in France, Italy, Germany, etc., the God, Christ, as well as his Mother is described in the old pictures to be black. The infant God in the arms of his black mother, his eyes and drapery white, is, himself, perfectly black. If the reader doubts my word he may go the Cathedral at Moulins—to the famous Chapel of the Virgin of Loretto, to the Church of the Annunciata; the Church of St. Lazaro, or the Church of St. Stephen of Genoa; to St. Francisco at Pisa; to the Church at Brixen in the Tyrol, and that at Padua; to the Church of St. Theodore at Munich, in the last two of which the whiteness of the eyes and teeth and the studied redness of the lips are observable; to a church and to the Cathedral at Augsburg, where are a black Virgin and child as large as life; to the Borghese Chapel, Maria Maggiore; to the Pantheon; to a small Chapel of St. Peter's on the right hand side on entering near the door; and, in fact to almost innumerable other churches in countries professing the Romish religion."[11]

These icons and statues receive the highest veneration from religious devotees. Hundreds of thousands make the annual pilgrimage to the *Shrine of the Black Madonna* at Alt-Otting in West Germany. Not only is this shrine and others like it Black in color but many of the wooden stone images dating as far back as 800 to 1,000 years or more are "completely Negro" in features. Says Rogers:

"The faces of these images are black and of Negroid type, particularly the Madonnas of Constuchan in Tolers and the Mother of God statue in Alto-Otting in Bavaria near Munich, which was brought from Palestine more than 1,000 years ago by Von Heiligers Lande."[12]

Many believe that through contact with these images one can be healed of sickness and diseases, and there have been many published reports to that effect. *The Black Virgin of Kazan*, also called "the miracle Ikon of Holy Russia," is noted for the alleged miracles it has performed. It is an ancient painting of the Madonna and infant Jesus dating back to the twelfth century.

In the book *Mary Portrayed*, Vincent Cronin observes: "France alone in sixteenth century possessed one hundred and ninety Black Madonnas...In the Black Madonna figures Jesus is usually represented as a little 'black bambino' in his mother's arms, and as such 'was the pet image of the Italian Church.' "[13]

Sometimes, Cronin continues, He is pictured as an adult; for instance, on "A coin of Justinian II in the British Museum"[14] which "shows Christ with the same tightly curled hair as that of the earlier Buddhas."[15] According to J. A. Rogers: *"The Cambridge Encyclopedia* says: 'What ever was the fact, this coin places beyond doubt the belief that Jesus Christ was a Negro.' "[16]

The mention of a Black Messiah and a Black Madonna in historical records, along with legends about them, is too frequent to be easily dismissed. These representations have persisted from ancient times to the present.

Even, as we have seen, in Europe.

How can this be? If, as we have also seen, Whites from their earliest times have painted Jesus white, both visually and spiritually, how can the seeming contradiction of a Black Messiah and Black Madonna exist on the same continent at the same time?

One answer leads to an area of neglected Black history: the formidable presence of Blacks in early Europe.

New research by scholars, such as has been published in the *Journal of African Civilizations*, edited by Professor Ivan Van Sertima, confirms much of the work of J.A. Rogers and other researchers. The contemporary scholars have shown that Black people were not only present in Europe, but in many areas and for many eras were most influential as builders, thinkers, leaders—and as objects of religious reverence.

American Perspectives

Blacks' presence in the Americas, and their subsequent belief in Christianity, adds further credence to the view of God in African form.

In *Introduction to African Civilizations*, John G. Jackson quotes A. Hyatt Verril:

" 'In the little church at Esquipultas, Guatemala, is the image of the Black Christ to which thousands of Indians journey annually from all parts of Central America, and even from Mexico and South America.' "[17]

Verill continues:

" 'Moreover, among many of the Indians, the Black Christ is referred to in private as Ekchuah or Hunabku (the former, the Mayan god of merchants, husbandmen and travellers; the latter, the godfather of supreme deity of the Mayas), often prefixed with the Spanish Cristo (Christ), as Christo Ekchuah or as Christo

Hunabku.' "[18]

In 1975, *Los Angeles Times* reporter Stanley Meisler wrote from Portobelo, Panama, that "Every Oct. 21, an odd grouping of thousands of purple-clad penitents and of fun lovers descends on the town to celebrate the procession of the Black Christ."[19] The image which is carried in the front of the procession is a "wooden sculpture of Christ, carved in dark wood either in the 17th or 18th centuries."[20] Reputed to have been carried there on a Spanish ship, it also is reputed to possess special miraculous powers, thereby inspiring the development of legends and practices, reports Meisler.

According to Angustia DeSus Critos, in *Mexico*, there are many images of the Black Christ in Mexico, "but perhaps the best known is that venerated in the Cathedral of Mexico as the 'Senor del Veneno.' "[21] Rogers quotes Riva-Palacio as saying: " 'The Mexicans recall a Negro God, Ixtlilton, which means black-faced,' "[22] and the *Cambridge Encyclopedia* of the time reads: " 'Quetzalcoatl, the Mexican Messiah, was also black and woolly-haired.' "[23]

There is a famous Black Christ located in the Phillipines, which is believed to have been taken there from Europe.

Most likely, there are many more interesting and significant artistic and symbolic images of a Black Messiah yet undiscovered in Central and South America, the Caribbean, and other islands of the seas.

The appearance of Black messianic consciousness in the United States dates back to the pre-Civil War era. During this period and in this setting, Blacks experienced the physical and mental abuse of slavery and its parallel propaganda denigrating all that was black. Their emerging kinship with Christ provided a vehicle to combat these physical and mental burdens. Two important examples from this era demonstrate this point.

Walker's *Appeal* was published in 1829 and Nat Turner's rebellion occurred only two years later in 1831. Both men were obviously influenced by the liberation motif of the Gospel message. Walker's fiery message, in which he spoke of hypocritical Whites who claimed to be Christian and yet treated Blacks like animals, relied heavily on his urgent belief in "the day of our redemption from the abject wretchedness...when we shall be enabled, in the most extended sense of the word, to stretch forth our hands to the LORD our God...."[24] This redemptive time, Walker foresaw, would be one in which "the God of the armies...will give [Blacks]... a Hannibal"[25] who would lead what Walker viewed as a battle of liberation from White oppression.

Turner's experience especially was characterized by a messianic consciousness or sense of divine mission. He claimed to have been shown in a vision things that happened before his birth, to which he added:

"And my father and mother strengthened me in this my first impression, saying in my presence, I was intended for some great purpose, which they had always thought from certain marks on my head and breast...."[26] Inasmuch as Turner's liberation of Blacks involved slaying numerous Whites, in the minds of his victims and other Whites, of course, he was considered a maniacal fanatic instead of a messiah.

A correlation between Black consciousness and the developing pattern of belief in a Black Christ may be presumed to have existed among Blacks in the United States during the period after the Civil War. From the standpoint of tradition, perhaps even Father Divine's acceptance of God in Black flesh in the twentieth century is attributable to a subconscious predisposition among the masses to sanction messianic beliefs which contradicts typical White representations of Christ.

In the 1920s, Marcus Garvey of the Universal Negro Improvement Association (UNIA) and Archbishop George Alexander McGuire of the African Orthodox Church advocated the elimination of all white images of Christ and the Madonna. This church canonized Jesus as the "Black man of sorrows," which is a variant of the concept of the "suffering servant of the Lord."

At the UNIA 1924 convention in New York, McGuire commanded that all white pictures of Jesus and Mary in Black homes and churches be torn down and burned and "Then let us start our Negro painters getting busy...and supply a black Madonna and a black Christ for the training of our children."[27] One Black woman associated with the Movement is alleged to have offered him five dollars for disclosing to her who Christ really was, because she knew that "no white man would ever die on the cross for..."[28] her. Interestingly, reactions to Garvey's and McGuire's concept of God and Christ as Black were similar in tone to earlier reactions to Bishop Henry M. Turner's "Negro" God. In about 1889 a White member of the press wrote in the *Observer:*

"Bishop Turner of the African Methodist Church says, 'that

God is a Negro.' The Good Bishop has been represented as one of the ablest men of his race and we thought justly so, for he is not only an intelligent thinker, but upon all subjects connected with his people his reasoning is profound, and in most instances unanswerable, but he is evidently becoming demented if he used the language attributed to him."[29]

The Observer's labeling of Turner as "demented" was more characteristic of the mockeries of the White press than of the Black press. But in Garvey's case it was the popular and influential Black journalist, George S. Schuyler, who ties in this "vagary" of a Black Diety to the eventual downfall of the UNIA. Another important Black figure of the times, Kelly Miller, was even more condescending. Miller responded:

"Marcus Garvey some little while ago shocked the spiritual sensibilities of the religious world by suggesting that the Negro should paint God Black...the idea was revolting even to the Negro."[30]

It should be noted that, whereas Garvey's appeal was mostly among the oppressed, impoverished masses, Miller and especially Schuyler belonged to the Black middle class establishment.

It was of this period, which coincided with the Harlem Renaissance, that Roi Ottley, in "New World A-Coming", wrote "...and more than one painter did a 'Black Christ' in oils."[31]

During this era, when the fermenting racial consciousness among Blacks—who were the victims of racist post-World War I atrocities—emerged in the vigorous artistic and literary output of figures such as Claude McKay, Langston Hughes and Countee Cullen. It was Hughes who wrote "Christ in Alabama": Christ is a nigger,

> Beaten and black,
> Oh, bare your back!
> Mary is His mother;
> Mammy of the South,
> Silence your mouth.
> God is His father:
> White Master above
> Grant Him your love.
> Most holy bastard
> Of the bleeding mouth,
> Nigger Christ
> On the cross
> Of the South.[32]

But it was Countee Cullen, W.E.B. BuBois' son-in-law, whose poetry exemplified most the inner struggle among Blacks for identity as it related to Christianity and their rightful place in it. Cullen's fluctuation between faith and fatalism, submission and rebellion, was explicitly revealed in "Heritage," a poem in his book *Color:*

Ever at Thy glowing altar
Must my heart grow sick and falter,
Wishing He I served were black,
Thinking then it would not lack
Precedent of pain to guide it,
Let who would or might deride it;
Surely then this flesh would know
Yours had borne a kindred woe.
Lord, I fashion dark gods, too,
Daring even to give You
Dark despairing features where
Crowned with dark rebellious hair,
Patience wavers just so much as
Mortal grief compels, while touches
Quick and hot, of anger, rise
To smitten cheek and weary eyes.
Lord, forgive me if my need
Sometimes shapes a human creed.[33]

Another poem by Cullen, "The Black Christ," published in Paris in 1928, reveals something of the psychological ordeal typical of Black consciousness at that time. Anger, frustration and skepticism were rampant in the Black community, brought about in part by the scourge of lynching which occurred in the United States during the years immediately after World War I. In the poem, Cullen argues:

God, if He was, kept to His skies,
And left us to our enemies...
A man was lynched last night.
"Why?" Jim would ask, his eyes star-bright.
A white man struck him; he showed fight,
Maybe God thinks such things are right."[34]

"The Black Christ" is a story about two brothers in the South. One of them, Jim, has been lynched for killing a White man. Christ is identified as Jim, who dies and then reappears, as in the Resurrection; then the other brother speaks thusly:

"No more," I cried, "this is too much
For one mad brain to stagger through."
For he stood in utmost view
Whose death I had been witness to;
But now he breathed; he lived, he walked;
He questioned me to know what art
Had made his enemies depart.[35]

Further research into the dominant themes, myths, images, and symbols of this period might show that Black writers and artists were even preoccupied with the Black Christ in one form or another.

In *Mark Twain and Southwestern Humor*, Kenneth S. Lynn says, "no other myth of the Negro has ever been so cherished by white America as the myth of the Black Christ."[36] He adds, "...the myth began in the self-consciousness of the slaves themselves."[37] Lynn believes that this "stereotype" was a true image but a false reality; that is, White people were deliberately led to believe that Blacks inherently possessed a superior Christian or Christlike humanity, morality and spirituality over their White slaveholders.

The central figure in Harriet Beecher Stowe's famous novel of 1852, *Uncle Tom's Cabin*, became the prototype of the White "vision" of Christlike virtue and behavior of enslaved and oppressed Blacks. Stowe's impact on and impetus for the abolition movement, immediately preceding the Civil War, may be summarized in Lynn's statement that:

"...if the Negro was a Black Christ, then slavery was daily crucifixion, and the moral acquiescence in that crucifixion by an allegedly Christian people was at least equivalent to the sin of Pilate.."[38] There is a basic human need for symbols and myths; they are a normal part of any culture. Black people have them just like all people do, because they nourish basic needs deep within the human mind and soul. S. P. Fullinwider also subscribes to the belief that "the myth of the Black Christ" has been a determining factor in the development of formal ideas and ideologies related to Black people. Only, differently, he views it from the standpoint of the Black man's image of himself.

In Fullinwider's *The Mind and Mood of Black America*, "myth" and "the sociological imagination" are shown to have engaged in a historical dialogue or dialectic. In Kenneth Boulding's words, "The image not only makes society, society continually remakes the image."[39]

In sum, myths must inevitably confront counter-myths, images, counter-images, resulting in revised myths and images which are syntheses of both past and present representations. Many Blacks have attacked and modified the Christlike myth as being distortional and destructive to a proper order of psychological and sociological realities.

W.E.B DuBois, whose influential career covered more than seventy years—from the 1890s to the 1960s—stood in the middle of this dialogue. Earlier he advocated the view of the messianic character and vocation of the Black community, but eventually he embraced Marxism with its class analysis of racial and socioeconomic problems. According to Fullinwider, DuBois, even with his strong rational and empiricist orientation, continued to manifest the influence of the Black Christ idea. Fullinwider notes:

"Like the religious radicals he revolted against the Christ-like Negro—no fit character for the new militancy—yet this same Christ-like Negro was the absolute to which he clung. The Christlike image together with its mission ideology was his integrating myth—it gave meaning to a world which was beginning to be described as chaos."[40]

As an intellectual giant and a prolific writer, DuBois gave ample expression to his "integrating myth" in both prose and poetry. Three short stories and one poem published in Darkwater in 1920 reflect DuBois' romance with this ideal messianic image. In "The Second Coming," a Black infant is born in a stable in Georgia, where three high ranking religious officials were invited by the governor of the state to a wedding feast. Only the Black bishop from New Orleans and the Japanese priest from San Francisco remained to acknowledge this manifestation of the Second Coming of Christ; the White bishop from New York turned away to attend wedding festivities.[41]

In "Jesus Christ in Texas," a mulatto stranger (Christ in disguise) is recognized by a child, a Black servant, a nurse, an escaped convict, and by the hounds chasing the convict; the other more affluent members in the story were not quite able to perceive who He was.[42]

"The Call" tells about a King who sat on a Great White Throne who needed someone to carry out a special errand. A Black woman responds but then demurs, giving as her excuse that she is Black. The king then reveals the color of his skin which also is

27

Black.[43]

In "The Riddle of the Sphinx," DuBois reveals his steadfast attachment to the futuristic dimension of the myth of the Black Messiah:

Who raised the fools to their glory,
But black men of Eqypt and Ind,
Ethiopia's sons of the evening,
Indians and yellow Chinese,
Arabian children of morning,
And mongrels of Rome and Greece,
   Ah, well!
And they that raised the boasters
Shall drag them down again, —
Down with the theft of their thieving
And murder and mocking of men;
Down with their barter of women
And laying and lying of creeds;
Down with their cheating of childhood
And drunken orgies of war, —
down
down
deep down,
Till the devil's strength be shorn,
Till some dim, darker David, a-hoeing of his corn,
And married maiden, mother of God,
Bid the black Christ be born![44]

Prejudicial and ethnocentric Western color symbolism in the United States, perhaps more than in any other country, translates into very concrete and malicious expressions of racism. Racist beliefs and practices of White "Christians" in this country have contributed to the development of a critical distance with which Blacks have learned to approach the White Christ figure. In "Artists Portray a Black Christ" is this statement:

"In Cedric Dover's book, *American Negro Art*, there is not a single illustration showing Christ or the Madonna and Child. It is not that the black artists were not religious. They painted preachers and church services, spiritual singers and baptism. But they seldom portrayed the key figure of Christianity—Christ himself."[45]

The article further suggests that the more Blacks in the U.S. began to conceive of the possibility that Jesus was Black, the more they portrayed Him as such. Allan Rohan Crite's drawings, done as early as 1948—before the 1960s renaissance in Black arts and letters—are examples of these "new" portrayals. In the introduction to Crite's *Three Spirituals From Earth to Heaven*, Roland Hayes, the world-renowned singer, says:

"Mr. Crite takes his inspiration, it seems, from the precedents of ancient stained glass windows and paintings in triptych form. Substituting black and white for color, he has achieved a distinctive style which gives the world a new token of the endowments of the Negro race."[46]

When Crite's book was published it was "new," indeed, to see Christ in the same dark image as the "darkies" who were regularly being hounded, mistreated and even lynched.

More recently, Black artists who have produced representations of the Black Christ and Madonna are Leroy Clark, Oliver Parson, Douglas R. Williams, Otto Neal, Omar Lama, Timothy Washington, Murray DePillars, Alvin Hollingsworth, Keithen Carte, Paul Davis and Jon Onye Lockard. Their works are exhibited at Howard University Divinity School; First Baptist Church, Melrose Park, Illinois; St. Dominic's Catholic Church, Chicago; St. Cecelia Catholic Church, Detroit; Church of the Jesu, Philadelphia; the Shrine of the Black Madonna, and many other locations.

DeVon Cunningham's mural in St. Cecelia includes a 24-foot portrayal of Jesus Christ in the midst of a throng of angels who represent a variety of racial types. The sculptured work located in the Church of the Jesu by artists Santiago and Jesu Rivas shows the Black Messiah crucified on a telephone pole wedged between tall tenements.

Glaton Dowdell's *Black Madonna and Child* is located in Detroit's Shrine of the Black Madonna, where Rev. Albert Cleage, founder of the Black Christian Nationalist Movement, presides. Cleage was catapulted to fame after publishing *The Black Messiah* in 1969 in support of his view that the historical Jesus of Nazareth was literally of African ancestry. With the development of Black Theology under such authors as Cleage and Dr. James H. Cone, the prediction that Blacks would increasingly portray Christ as also Black if they could conceive of Him as such, became a reality among larger number of Blacks.

This "new" reality, as depicted in the artistic creations previously mentioned, has been echoed in recent generalized representations of the Black Christ that may be found in a variety of literary creations. For instance, "The Boy Who Painted Christ

Black" is a short story by John Henrik Clarke which tells about a precocious young Black boy who was ridiculed and denounced by a White superintendent of schools for painting Christ as a Black man. The Black principal of the school, who defended the boy by saying, "I don't think the boy is so far wrong in painting Christ Black," was relieved of his duties.[47] Clarke's story, while expressing the timely message of the emerging relationship felt by Blacks to the Black Messiah, also points out that a price was to be paid by Black people for their increasingly assertive consciousness.

As has been explored in this chapter, this developing consciousness came about over a period of several centuries and in the widely varied settings of Africa, Eurasia, and the Americas. Kimpa Vita maintained that Jesus was African, just as the followers of the Orunmia movement proclaimed. Throughout West Germany, France, Italy and other European nations, the existence and popularity of Black Madonna and Black Messiah shrines sustain the notion that believers have an alternative figure on whom to base a different pattern of beliefs than the White Christ figure. This ironic occurrence—of Black Messiah and Madonna figures among the very same people whose leaders were responsible for the kidnapping of Africans and their enslavement—continued its ironic path to the Americas. There, particularly in the United States, the development took place by Blacks of a conscious effort to conceive and portray Christ as Black.

The American irony is undeniable. The very same situation in which existed the atrocities of slavery, lynch mobs, and the everyday denigration of anything and anyone Black—American racism—became the impetus for creating alternative representations of the Redeemer. These representations have included the stories and poetry created by Harlem Renaissance authors such as Langston Hughes, Countee Cullen and W.E.B. DuBois, who reflective of their chronological context, were not yet willing to view Christ Jesus in a different light than the one portrayed by White racists. One the other hand, another movement was gathering influence during the 1920s and this movement—as led by Marcus Garvey and Archbishop McGuire—advocated Blacks' belief in Jesus as Black. As we shall see in the next chapter, the struggle to believe in the Black Messiah addressed a powerful need with an equally powerful challenge in store for Blacks.

Footnotes
1. Bengt Sundkler, "Bantu Messiah and White Christ," *Practical Anthropology* 7 (1967): pp. 171-2.
2. Ibid., p. 175.
3. Marie-Louise Martin, *Kimbangu: An African Prophet and His Church* (Oxford: Basil Blackwell, 1975), p. 14.
4. Ibid., p. 15.
5. Vittorio Lanternari, *Religions of the Oppressed: A Study of Modern Messianic Cults* (New York: Alfred A. Knopf, Inc., 1960, 1963), pp. 53-4.
6. Snowden, p. 171.
7. Arna Lehmann, *Christian Art in Africa and Asia* (St. Louis: Concordia Publishing House, 1969), p. 48.
8. Ibid., p. 172.
9. J. A. Rogers, *Sex and Race: Negro-Caucasian Mixing in All Ages and All Lands,* Vol. I, *The Old World* (New York: Helga M. Rogers, 1952, 1967), p. 265.
10. Ibid., pp. 265-6.
11. Ibid., p. 274.
12. Ibid., p. 275.
13. Vincent Cronin, *Mary Portrayed* (London: Darton, Longman and Todd, 1968), p. 141.
14. Ibid.
15. Ibid.
16. Rogers, *Sex and Race*, etc., Vol. I, p. 275.
17. John G. Jackson, *Introduction to African Civilizations* (Secaucus: The Citadel Press, 1970), pp. 255-6.
18. Ibid.
19. Stanley Meiser, "Panamanian Home of Black Christ", *"Los Angeles Times,* (29 December 1975, Monday, Part 1), pp. 10-1.
20. Ibid.
21. Angustia Desus Cristos, Mexico, n.d., n.p., p. xxxvii.
22. Rogers, *Sex and Race*, etc., Vol. I, p. 270.
23. Ibid.
24. Lerone Bennett, Jr., "The Fanon of the Nineteenth Century," *Pioneers in Protest* (Chicago: Johnson Publishing Company, 1968), p. 78.
25. Ibid.

26. Herbert Aptheker, *Nat Turner's Slave Rebellion* (New York: Grove Press, Inc., 1966), p. 133.

27. David E. Cronon, *Black Moses: The Story of Marcus Garvey* and the *Universal Negro Improvement Association* (Madison: University of Wisconsin Press, 1955, 1969), p. 179.

28. Ibid.

29. John H. Bracey, Jr., Meier and Rudwick, eds., *Black Nationalism in America* (New York: The Bobbs-Merrill Company, Inc., 1970), p. 154.

30. Ibid., pp. 181-2.

31. Roi Ottley, *New World A-Coming* (Arno Press and the New York Times, 1943, 1968, rprt), p. 73.

32. Langston Hughes, *The Panther and the Lash: Poems of Our Times* (New York: Alfred A. Knopf, Inc., 1969), p. 37.

33. Countee Cullen, "Heritage," *Color* (New York: Harper and Bros., 1925), pp. 36-41.

34. Countee Cullen, *The Black Christ* (New York: Harper and Bros., 1928, 1929), p. 77.

35. Ibid., p. 107.

36. Kenneth S. Lynn, *Mark Twain and Southwestern Humor* (Boston: Little, Brown and Company, 1959), p.5.

37. Ibid.

38. Ibid., p. 111.

39. Kenneth E. Boulding, *The Image* (Ann Arbor: The University of Michigan Press, 1956, 1969), p. 64.

40. S. P. Fullinwider, *The Mind and Mood of Black America: Twentieth Century Thought* (Homewood: The Dorsey Press, 1969), p. 48.

41. W. E. B. DuBois, *Darkwater: Voices from Within the Veil* (New York: Schocken Books, 1920, 1969), pp. 104-8.

42. Ibid., pp. 123-33.

43. Ibid., pp. 161-2.

44. Ibid., p. 54.

45. "Artists Portray a Black Christ," *Ebony*, XXVI, No. 6 (April 1971), p. 177.

46. Allan Rohan Crite, *Three Spirituals from Earth to Heaven* (Cambridge, Mass.: Harvard University Press, 1948), n.p.

47. John Henrik Clarke, "The Boy Who Painted Christ Black," *Brothers and Sisters: Modern Stories by Black Americans*, ed., Arnold Adoff (New York: Dell Publishing Company, Inc., 1970, 1975), pp. 55-62.

CHAPTER 4

The Psychological Significance of Jesus Christ's Image on the Black Psyche

The Current State of the Black Psyche

The image of Jesus Christ as White festers at the heart of White racism, the belief in and/or practice of racial superiority. It can take many forms: individual or institutional, systematic or systemic, overt or covert, conscious or unconscious or even subconscious. It plays itself out in the forms of prejudice, discrimination, segregation, oppression, exploitation, and genocide.

White racism is supported by and entrenched in the belief that Jesus Christ was White. The motive for aryanizing Christ must be regarded as a racist distortion of Christian symbols and a betrayal of basic human sentiments. However, ego satisfaction and ethnocentrism, in and of themselves, do not necessarily demand a sense of superiority and mastery over other persons or groups. Therefore, how did this notion of Jesus Christ as White come about? Does God really intend for humanity to perceive of Jesus as White, or are there other forces at work? Why is His image so important? These and other questions need to be explored by first viewing the current state of the Black psyche, since it is that substance which shapes and defines Blacks' perspective of Christ's racial image, as well as their own self-esteem.

Jesus Christ is God's own symbolization of Himself and the ideal human self in one, God's own abstract-concrete picture, God's own visual poetic masterpiece, God's perfect work of art, God's self-image. But cultural beliefs about Christ among humans almost invariably surface in the form of concrete semi-subjective symbols; hence the White Christ. Baltazar reveals an awareness of this human tendency:

"An even more significant influence of color symbolism was the operative process of deliberately whitening or bleaching the center of the Christian Faith, namely, Jesus Christ, from a Semitic to an Aryan person to which the entire history of Western painting bears witness."[1]

In 1940, eminent Black sociologist E. Franklin Frazier sought to understand this distortion. Frazier and his team of researchers interviewed Black boys and girls and asked them if Jesus was a White man.

They replied:

"Pictures I've seen of Him are all white so I just took for granted He was a white man."

"It wouldn't do for Him to have been Negro...I don't suppose Christ would have had many Negro followers had He been a Negro."

"The Lord is white. In all the Sunday School books and books I see around with His picture in them, He seems to be white. He always has a straight, narrow nose and long, flowing hair."

"I've never given it a thought; though I suppose He was a white man—all the pictures we see of Him make Him a white man."

"If by chance He is anything else, the white people have taken great pains to make Him a white man throughout these many, many years."[2]

Art, then, functions as a kind of "visual preaching," frequently with the express purpose giving concrete form to abstract or theological notions. Artistic productions at the very least reflect and reinforce individual and collective convictions. In "Art, Religion, and Education," F. Graeme Chalmers says:

"The survey of literature indicates that one of the main functions of art as communication is to reinforce belief, custom and values by supplementing the abstractions of belief with emotion provoking symbolism."[3]

Much of what goes on in the lives of Blacks with regard to their racial and color consciousness is, of course, the function of that level of existence known as the unconscious. Most people are not aware of the cultural influences which affect their personality and behavior patterns. Personal, interpersonal, and social relations are expressed often from out of the depth of the "cultural unconscious." Rollo May, in "The Significance of Symbols," says:

"...an individual's self-image is built up of symbols. Symbolizing is basic to such questions as personal identity. For the individual experiences himself as a self in terms of symbols which arise from three levels at once; those from archaic and archetypal depths within himself, symbols arising from the personal events of his psychological and biological experience, and the general symbols and values which obtain in his culture."[4]

The pyschological implications of this distorted and emotion-provoking symbolism have been treated in various ways. For example, in *Art as Therapy with Children*, Edith Kramer points to the role that art plays as a means of "supporting the ego, fostering the development of a sense of identity, and promoting maturation in general."[5]

A ten-year-old Black child who suffered from masochistic tendencies was one of the student-patients of whom she gives the following account.

"When the time of his discharge approached, Larry devoted many of his art lessons to religious paintings. Most of them were conventional renderings of Christ or of angels. His last painting, Christ with the bleeding heart, was more expressive. The Christ figure, depicted as a light-skinned Negro, resembled Larry. It seemed as if the pressures of imminent discharge had brought forth more profound feelings. The bloodiness of the heart suggested persisting sado-masochistic tendencies now expressed as religious symbolism."[6]

Eldridge Cleaver, in *Soul on Ice*, suggests that Black women who long "to be rocked in the arms of Jesus (the white Christ) will burn for the blue eyes and white arms of the All-American boy."[7] The highly sex-oriented Cleaver merely adds a theological corollary to Franz Fanon's psycho-sexual analytic theories. In this connection, Black theoretician Franz Fanon says:

"If one wants to understand the racial situation psychoanalytically, not from a universal standpoint but as it is experienced by individual consciousness, considerable importance must be given to sexual phenomena."[8]

The point here is that close identification with Christ (Black or White) has socio-psychological implications at the unconscious as well as the conscious level.

These implications, inasmuch as they influence the Black psyche, also contribute to Blacks' sense of pride and their self-image and self-esteem. All these subjects have received much attention from many quarters of Black and White America. Dr. Alvin Poussaint, a Black psychiatrist associated with Harvard University, observed:

"The most tragic, yet predictable, part of all this is that the Negro has come to form his self-image and self-concept on the basis of what white racists have prescribed. Therefore, black men and women learn quickly to hate themselves and each other more than their white oppressor. There is abundant evidence that racism has left almost irreparable scars on the psyche of Afro-Americans that burden them with an unrelenting, painful anxiety that drives the psyche to reach out for a sense of identity and self-esteem."[9]

Poussaint says that Black children, particularly, learn to hate themselves at very early ages. He points to studies that reveal their preference for white dolls over black ones. According to Poussaint, "One study reported that Negro children in their drawings tend to show Negroes as small, incomplete people and whites as strong and powerful."[10]

Without stretching the point too far, one might also conclude that for a Black person to love the White version of God is to hate self (Black self) because in Western color symbolism white and black connote polar opposites.

With reference to the ill effects of Western color symbolism on Blacks, Bishop Henry M. Turner of the AME Church made the following statement in 1898:

"This is one of the reasons we favor African emigration, or Negro nationalization, wherever we can find a domain, for as long as we remain among the Whites, the Negro will believe that the devil is black and that he (the Negro) bears no resemblance to Him, and the effect of such a sentiment is contemptuous and degrading, and one-half of the Negro race will be trying to be white men's scullions in order to please the whites; and the time they should be giving to the study of such things as will dignify and make our race great, will be devoted to studying about how unfortunate they are in not being white."[11]

More conclusively, in *Christianity, Islam, and the Negro Race,* Edward W. Blyden quotes an even earlier statement that Turner made in *The American Methodist Episcopal Church Review* in 1885: " 'No race or people can rise and manufacture better conditions while they hate and condemn themselves. A man must believe he is somebody before he is acknowledged to be somebody.' "12

In *Christian Faith in Black and White,* Warner R. Traynham suggests that there is indeed a psychological correlation between Black self-acceptance and the acceptance of a Black Christ. In Traynham's words, "yet hardly ever is Christ depicted...as Black. The reason, I believe, is that as a group the Black community has never completely accepted itself."13

Traynham further observes: "...there is some talk in the Black community about the images in the Black church—images (pictures or statues) still teach, of course. It has been asserted that Christ should be shown as Black since every people depict him as their own and because a white Christ imply that God is white and encourage the traditional subservience of Black people to whites, who occupy all other seats of authority."14

In summary, Langdon Gilkey, in *Naming the Whirlwind: The Renewal of God Language,* addresses the related issue of the dilemma of freedom in a secularized society like that of the United States: "...insofar as I am really free to be myself, so much the more am I forced to find a model, an image of man's existence which I wish to embody."15

Similarly, the liberation of the Black psyche means there must be the creation of a new psychic structure compatible with Black reality, Black hope, Black culture, Black spirit. Until it is identified with a positive psychic character, Blackness is left without a structure of reality in which to anchor its universalism.

The Black Liberator, Jesus, provides a model whose similarity to ethno-cultural and historical Blackness makes Him compatible to the Black experience today. Indeed, the experience of Black reality is conditioned by how one perceives reality: the experience of the reality of Christ, therefore, is conditioned by identification with His perceived Blackness.

Identification with Christ

Conscious and/or unconscious identification with Christ, the ultimate symbol of perfect divinity and humanity, may be the single most important factor in the development of some individuals' self-image. The real Jesus Christ, as a transcendant reference point, does not fit into the color vocabulary of Western Christianity, with its denigration of Black and exultation of White. Nevertheless, these distorted renditions of Christ continue to dominate the mind of the Western world.

In another essay entitled "The Nature of the Symbol," Erich Kahler defines symbol as a union of divergent elements:

"The symbol is something concrete and specific that is intended to convey something spiritual or general, either as an indicating sign, i.e., an act of pointing, or as an actual representation in which the dynamic division of the sign is abolished: that which points, that which is pointed to, and the act of pointing, have become one and the same. The Greek word symballein, from which 'symbol' derives, means: 'to bring together,' or, 'to come together.' The symbolic sign brings together, the symbolic representation is a coming together, to the point of complete fusion, of the concrete and the spiritual, the specific and the general."[16]

As for me and my house, we will serve the Lord.

In "The Function of Symbols in Religious Experience," F. W. Dillistone says "...there is only one non-symbolic reality—God Himself."[17] If this is true, then Christ as a human being created in the image of God is the best symbolic representation of God. But Christ is also God; therefore He is "the point of complete fusion" of the visible and the invisible, the human and the Divine. He is the ideal image, the unifying concept, the exemplary pattern of the dual expression of Divine-human experience fused into a single reality. As such Christ is the one symbolic representation in which humankind may identify and understand the unique relationship between the spirituality of God and the materiality of the self.

In "Symbolism and the Jewish Faith," Abraham Joshua Heschel says: "The one symbol of God is man, every man."[18]

Heschel believes everyone should obey the dictum to treat themselves as symbols of God. On the other hand, Christianity has elevated Jesus above the status of a mere symbol to the symbol of Deity; that is, the ultimate symbol of the Ultimate Reality. In short, in a society in which Christ is the primary symbol of Supreme Value—the master-image of God and man—all individual self-images will be greatly affected by this cultural force, either consciously or unconsciously.

European cultural imposition and imperialism are characterized by the way they have established definitive ways of acting and thinking for all of its subordinated peoples.

White Christology is simply the expression of this dominance in the field of theoretical and practical theology. Under this belief, anything or anybody not resembling the European standard cannot be considered of value. Thus, only a Caucasian type could be acceptable in the portrayal of Christ. This identification of Christ with a typical White appearance, therefore, excludes His identification with Blacks. At the same time it reinforces notions and feelings of superiority among those whose physical appearance most approximates the prevailing conception. On the question of White figures of Jesus as a symbol of their superiority, Malachi Martin, an authority on references to Jesus in Jewish and Islamic sources, observes:

"As a multipurpose figure, Jesus became all things to all men: for white Western believers, a symbol of their superiority and a justification of their excesses; for Jews, a repellent figure replete with Christian hate; for Muslims, a supreme prophet, born of a virgin, second only to Mohammed; for Africans and Asians, a symbol for Western colonialism and power. What Jesus achieved and achieves became visibly identified with 'Christianity.' And this 'Christianity' became synonymous and practically coterminous with white culture and Western civilization. All that had to end."[19]

Na'im Akbar in *Chains and Images of Psychological Slavery* comments:

"The person who looks up and sees his physical characteristics shared by the deity, begins to develop the idea that he is like that, or that God is like him. This is all right if one sees potential for growth within that idea; but the confusion of the physical attributes with the very nature of God, begins to make the person feel that his particular physical features have endowed him with automatic claims to divinity. Such a person can begin to believe in his own mind, that:

'I am God, I am the Deity, I am the Creator.'

He begins to believe that the blond hair and blue eyes that are on the portrait are his qualifications for divinity. This begins to cultivate an ego maniac."[20]

Iman Waarith Deen Muhammad raises this penetrating question: "What would happen to the minds of Caucasian people if Black people would suddenly come into power with their mentality, with their love for their religion? What would happen if nappy-headed, Black Jesuses were put all over their land and throughout their homes, and in all of their churches? What would happen to their minds over a period of three-hundred years if they kept coming to churches and seeing our image as their redeemer, seeing our image as their prophets, their apostles, their angels? They would be reduced to inferiority because the image before them of the supreme model of superiority would be Black and not White."[21]

If Christ is the perfect reflection of an infinitely holy God, then He is faith's most highly regarded sacred symbol. As such, it is extremely important that this embodied reflection of Supreme Holiness be guarded from distortions. If interpretations of Jesus affect faith and faith affects attitudes and behavior, and they do, then a Black or White representation of Jesus will have corresponding effects. Here Professor Rosemary Ruether's point is well taken:

"The pictures in the Sunday School books and the biblical

figures that paraded down the walls and the stained glass windows were uniformly Caucasian in features and coloring. There was little sense of the incongruity of this, not only for the self-image of the worshippers, but in terms of Biblical History itself!"[22]

While pointing to historical incongruities, Ruether also mentions the importance of being aware of self-imagery.

White representations of Christ found in many Black and White churches and homes must affect believers in some way. Black children, especially, growing up under that influence of images of Christ with White skin and Caucasian features, will find it difficult to disassociate them in later years. Emotional conditioning occasioned by associative learning may, indeed it often does, lead to a lifelong romance with and reverence for anyone who resembles those images. On the other hand, White Jesus images tend to achieve an inverse effect on Black children's self-image; since they are not White they are therefore unlike Christ; they are unholy.

In an article entitled "Racial Prejudice and the Black Self-Concept," Professor James A. Banks points to the usefulness of "significant others," particularly with reference to Black children. Banks is convinced that "Blacks should work to create new 'significant others' for Black children, and provide them with successful models with whom they can identify."[23] In "The World Through Mark's Eyes," Dr. Cynthia N. Separd, a professor of education, described her arduously long and distressful search for a way to help her son to resolve his identity problems. Finally, she concludes:

"I found a book about John Henry, with all the usual legendary verbiage. But it had pictures—pictures of John Henry as a big, black, and beautiful baby; pictures of a handsome, adventurous black youth; and then, a picture of a dynamic, virile, muscle-bound black man. John Henry, the steel-driving man: a beautiful portrayal of black maleness, bared to the waist, swinging that hammer with all his might. It is with THAT picture that my son finally identified: an uncompromising image of black masculinity."[24]

It is not difficult to understand why conventional graphic visages of Jesus Christ would be considered inappropriate for Blacks who are searching for "models" and "significant others" to identify with. It is difficult, however, to suppose that pictures of the legendary John Henry would have more identification potential, especially for Black Christians, than pictures of Jesus portrayed as a convincingly realistic Black figure.

Such graphic realism—portraying Jesus as Black and in His occupational role as a craftsman, a skilled carpenter and the like—might easily compete for the admiration of Black youth with negative images in the Black child's environment. At any rate, a Black Christ, as the focus of identification processes, might play a major role in the moral, religious, and psychological development of Black adults as well as children.

But is it possible to have a clear and rooted belief in self that is not connected to the world around you?

Only a mechanical, one-dimensional approach would insist on divorcing beliefs about self from moral, religious, ethical, and theological beliefs. Individual self-evaluations are partially related to religion in particular and to spiritual beliefs in general. In other words, how one views oneself is directly tied to how one views the culture one is in.

The process of identification operates on a broad spectrum of relationships, i.e., personal, interpersonal, social, and spiritual. In an article entitled "Identification Theory and Christian Moral Education," S. Anita Stauffer supplies the following definition of this phenomenon:

"Definitions of identification presuppose a relationship between a self and a model, commonly including one, two, or all three aspects: 1. a molding of the self after the model; 2. a belief by the self that he is similar in some way to the model; 3. a vicarious sharing by the self of the model's emotions."[25]

The second proposition cited in Stauffer's definition is of particular importance to our understanding of messianic imagery. Indeed, for Blacks to walk across the bridge from the Jesus of white symbolic distortions to Jesus as He was and is, Black imagery must necessarily be employed.

As interest in Black Theology continues to increase, especially in academic circles, more "critical concern" is being shown in the significance of the relationship between Western color symbolism and Black Christology.

On the christological continuum, at one end there are those whose views represent a henotheistic approach. At the other end are those who have a dogmatic religious, nationalist perspective. In the case of the former, Jesus is not considered to be Black in reality so much as in form or figure. Not much distinction can be made between their Black Jesus and the theatrical persona; that is, a White Jesus with a Black mask. But in the case of the latter, Jesus is seriously regarded as literally Black, either from an existential viewpoint or in terms of actual genetic constitution.

There is, of course, a lot of overlapping in the various interpretations; therefore, to place each writer in a particular school of thought would contribute more to confusion than to clarity. As Black Theology moves from the critical stage into the constructive stage, we can expect that more and more definitive arguments will be made on the subject of the Black Christ.

There is nearly unanimous consensus about the psychological significance of Jesus imagery. It would seem therefore, that the dialogue between Black Christology and Black psychology has just begun.

Black Power and the Black Messiah

We have surveyed numerous historical examples of Black Jesus imagery. We have also examined mythical and symbolic images, because our perspective has been that no clear and measurable distinction should exist between the historical Jesus on the one hand and the mythic and symbolic Jesus on the other. We believe this because the way we know the historical Jesus is through the way He is represented in art and symbol.

As Gerardus van der Leeuw asserts in *Sacred and Profane Beauty: the Holy in Art:*

"If man wants to achieve a real relationship with what is, it must first 'take place.' It is not enough that it simply be there, that it happen. It must first be imagined or represented, in order to really exist. 'The holy becomes valid only in the concrete situation of man.' We can express the holy only when we can see it as an image."[26]

Further, he says,

"There is no reality besides that which is consummated in an image. From this point the path leads us into the midst of theology, into the doctrine of the image of God."[27]

Just as theology begins with the image of God, so Black Theology begins with the Black image of God.

In 1966, during a civil rights march outside Greenwood, Mississippi, Stokely Carmichael (now Kwame Ture) introduced a slogan that would have a far-reaching impact on the Movement and, indeed, on America itself. In *Where Do We Go From Here?*, Martin Luther King, Jr. gives the following account:

"As we approached the city, large crowds of old friends and new turned out to welcome us. At a huge mass meeting that night, which was held in a city park, Stokely mounted the platform and after arousing the audience with a powerful attack on Mississippi justice, he proclaimed: 'what we need is black power.' Willie Ricks, the fiery orator of SNCC, leaped to the platform and shouted, 'What do you want?' The crowd roared, 'Black Power.' Again and again Ricks cried, 'What do you want?' and the response 'Black Power' grew louder and louder, until it had reached fever pitch."[28]

The new militancy, the new sense of Black nationhood, escalated into other variations of awareness such as "Black is Beautiful," and "I'm Black and I'm Proud," which swept across the country like wildfire. Watts, Newark, and Detroit went up in flames, betokening a newfound "courage to be"—the courage to be outspoken, assertive, aggressive, rebellious. Somewhere in the wake of all this "revolutionary" fervor, the hitherto conservative religious elements of the Black community also caught fire. Thus, Black Power as a force and as a symbol gave birth to a new Black theological consciousness.

Contemporary Black Theology may be said to have begun with the publication of Joseph Washington's *Black Religion* in 1964, a book that was partially responsible for the ensuing dialogue among religious thinkers, leaders and writers. However, it was Reverend Albert Cleage's *Black Messiah* (1969)[29] and Dr. James H. Cone's *Black Theology and Black Power* (1969)[30] that reintroduced the theme of the Black Christ into the theological arena, in particular, and into Black consciousness in general.

Apparently this contemporary theological phenomenon parallels the rise of Black Nationalist trends in America. As Blacks have shaken off their White images of themselves, they have at the same time shaken off a false image of Jesus.

Black Theology in the U.S. can trace its roots to the period before the Civil War. But it had its flowering around the same time as the Black Power movement of the late 1960s and 1970s. Though both Black Power and Black Theology have formal antecedents in the Civil Rights movement, there are distinctions between Black Power and Civil Rights.

First, Black Power, though less talked about these days,

emphasizes the long-lasting themes of Black economic and political unity and self-determination, as opposed to "integrationist" and "equal civil rights" approaches.

Second, Black Power reflects the wholehearted and uncritical reliance on the Judeo-Christian ethic as it is interpreted by Europeans. Civil rights advocates were all too willing to endorse this interpretation, without qualifications, so long as they could be accepted into the so-called American mainstream or American melting pot.

Third, Black Power does not limit itself to certain strategies and tactics. One notion it subscribes to is that of liberation "by any means necessary," instead of relying solely on reductionist legal and/or nonviolent strategies.

Fourth, Black Power supports Black Nationalism and internationalism, which may not be acceptable to those who cling vainly to American interpretations of brotherhood.

Black Theology, therefore, is concerned with the spiritual interpretation of the Black religious, cultural, economic, and political debate. Its primary objective, then, is the total spiritual and material liberation of all peoples of African descent.

Part of this debate concerns the implicit contradictions inherent in White Jesus imagery and Black self-imagery, versus Black Jesus imagery and White self-imagery. In a general sense, Black Christology is that category of theological analysis in which Christ is examined from a Black perspective.

The many Black theological perspectives on Jesus Christ include a broad cross section of Christological opinion. Although they do not all agree with one another, their proponents are among a larger body of persons who have formed a general consensus about the significance of the image and concept of a Black Christ.

C. Eric Lincoln, in *The Black Church Since Frazier*, refers to color as a significant factor in interpreting the essential character of God.

"Black theology is not necessarily a treatise on the color of God, but the nature of God as revealed through His color gradually became a principal theme of the theological interests of Blacks over the past hundred years, and is of critical concern today."[31]

This theological concern with God's color is tied to the idea of divine liberation for Blacks. It deals with the question of whether a person who is Black can identify with a God who is considered White. Again, if the incarnation of God is White, doesn't this mean that His behavior vis-à-vis Blacks will be the same or similar to the generally negative way a White person treats a Black one?

Just as general notions about Christ are at the center of biblical theology, so the Black Christ is at the heart of Black Theology. Hence, Black Christology, or the theological study of a Black incarnation of God, is of critical concern today.

According to Paul Tillich:

"Theology ... is the conceptual interpretation, explanation and criticism of symbols in which a special encounter between God and man has found expression. This is the basic statement about the relationship between theology and symbolism."[32]

From this definition, Black Theology is, or should be, engaged in creating, explaining, interpreting and criticizing Black messianic characterizations of God. Accordingly, many Black and some non-Black theologians who have published works on this theme reflect this "critical concern."

Albert A. Cleage Jr., perhaps more than most others, takes an uncompromising literalistic stance:

"When I say that Jesus was black, that Jesus was the black Messiah, I'm not saying, 'Wouldn't it be nice if Jesus was black?' or 'Let's pretend that Jesus was black,' I'm saying that Jesus WAS black. There never was a white Jesus."[33]

Cleage's historical analysis leads him to the conclusion that the biblical Jews comprised a Black or at least non-White nation suffering under the oppressive regime of a White nation (Rome), when Jesus appeared as the Black Liberator.

The variety of theological interpretations range from Cleage's exclusively Black conception to a type of henotheistic Christology which allows for all peoples to view and accept Christ as being in their own image, e.g., red, yellow, brown, white.

One of the mandates of Black Theology, according to James H. Cone, is to end the reign and worship of a White god in the Black community. Not to do so would be tantamount to accepting the doctrine of White supremacy and White racism for which it is the foundation. Without tongue in cheek, Cone asserts: "The White God is an idol, created by racists,... and we Black people must perform the iconoclastic task of smashing false images."[34]

Following the practice of Karl Barth and others, Cone takes

Christology as the focal point in his theology. In his opinion, "Christian theology begins and ends with Jesus Christ. He is the point of departure for everything to be said about God, man, and the world."[35]

In discussing the sources and norms of Black Theology, Cone says his Christology does not advocate the concept of a raceless, colorless, universal Christ. In fact, he conceives of the modern liberal emphasis on the universality of Christ as a sanction for orthodox theological racism in American churches. Insistence on the irrelevance of race and color in the figure of Christ simply discourages any effort to correct the way He has been portrayed for centuries.

Ben Ammi in *God the Black Man and Truth* observes: "Why is it that the problem of race only enters the picture when we begin discussing positive Black images? How could it be that all of these artists have had such a vivid imagination of all those characters being European? But none of them have ever imagined that those African Hebrews. . . were Black. . . . Now you even feel offended when someone suggests that the pictures be taken down and destroyed. When someone mentions the racist connotation of these pictures to European Christians or others, the favorite answer is, 'God doesn't have any color.' And worse yet, is when he turns around and implies that the one who raises the question is a racist."[36]

Cone's standard of measure is the Black Messiah who is the master key to unlock the mystery of religious experience. Moreover, Cone's conception of Blackness involves a dual meaning: first, it refers to race and color; second, it represents identification with oppressed peoples in their struggle for liberation. Put together, this conception means that Blacks and other people of color are the most oppressed and therefore directly related to the nature and mission of Jesus Christ, the visible manifestation of the God of the oppressed.

In Cone's book *God of the Oppressed,* he explains:

"Christ's blackness is both literal and symbolic. His blackness is literal in the sense that he truly becomes One with the oppressed Blacks, taking their suffering as his suffering and revealing that he is found in the history of our struggle, the story of our pain, and the rhythm of our bodies.

"Christ's blackness is the American expression of the truth of his parable about the Last Judgement: 'Truly, I say to you, as you

did it not to one of the least of these, you did it not to me'
(Matthew 25:45). The least in America are literally and symboli-
cally present in Black people."[37]

Cone does not take a position on Jesus' historical, hereditary
Blackness because the question most relevant to him is "Who is
Jesus Christ for us today?"[38] In the following statement Cone's
existential posture is clearly reflected: "Thinking of Christ as
non-black in the twentieth Century is as theologically impossible
as thinking of him as non-Jewish in the first Century."[39]

The above statement shows a crucial twist in Cone's theological interpretation. The divine nature, he says, consists of more
than just a conglomeration of attributes, e.g., love, mercy, compassion, justice, power: it involves His activity as well. Therefore
the divine presence may be identified by an awareness of those
persons, events, and movements in today's world in which love,
etc., are actively demonstrated. There is no need to speculate on
the whereabouts of Deity; if He is the "God of the oppressed,"
then, where the oppressed are is the focus of His self-disclosures.
Since Christ is the complete manifestation of divine presence and
power, as is God so is Christ. The incarnation is Deity revealing
Himself in a concrete historical situation of suffering and
oppression in Christ, the Liberator. The death and resurrection
of Jesus guarantees victory over sin and death, and the disconti-
nuance of slavery and oppression.

In *The Spirituals and the Blues*, Cone exclaims:

"If Jesus was not alone in His suffering, they were not alone in
their slavery. Jesus was with them! He was God's Black slave
who had come to put an end to human bondage. Herein lies the
meaning of the resurrection."[40]

If Christ is Black and identifies Himself with oppressed communities of people who are struggling for freedom and self-
determination, then the Black Power movement and Black radi-
calism are divinely inspired and sanctioned. Indeed, Blackness
becomes the prime medium or anointed symbol through which
divine holiness is disclosed.

Black consciousness is the consciousness of the holy, the experience of the higher mysteries, the subjective call to ultimate
concern and commitment. Furthermore, the Black community is
the locus of prophetic faith, apocalyptic hope and creative love;
the channel of miracles, exorcisms and healings. In Cone's words,
"Black is holy, that is, it is a symbol of God's presence in history

on the behalf of oppressed man."[41] And in the words of the Bible, "... God anointed Jesus of Nazareth with the Holy Ghost and with power: who went about doing good, and healing all that were oppressed of the devil" (Acts 10:38).

Rosemary Ruether in *Liberation Theology*, poses the question, "Is black theology just a new form of racial propaganda, making Christ in the image of black exclusivism?"[42]

Answering, she points to the necessity of maintaining a catholic spirit and the dangers involved in particularizing the gospel to meet the needs of a given ethnic group. She makes it clear, however, that God's universality is not an abstraction, and that revelation occurs in concrete, cultural, and historical circumstances.

According to Ruether, these notions of particularity and universality are complementary and not contradictory. Though God reveals Himself in the "unique context" of the Black experience, that revelation of the universal must not be interpreted in an exclusive manner; that is, a true grasp of divine revelation embodied in various particularizations of universal truth requires a cross-cultural approach or analysis. She explains:

"God is the God of all men, each in his own particularity and culture. So the Gospel rightfully comes to the black man in the form of a Black Messiah, not in an exclusivistic, racist sense, but in the sense of that historical context which gives to each people a salvation that encounters their situation."[43]

Professor Ruether's critical endorsement of the Black religio-cultural revolution is her way of accounting for and encouraging vehicles by which Black Messiahship may put in a strong appearance. This messianic appearance "... in the form of a Black Messiah," is born of cultural and theological integrity,struggle, and freedom.

Indeed, insofar as theology remains the reflection of a dominant White culture, it will tend to obscure or obstruct authentic messianic conceptions and perceptions emerging out of indigenous Black theological culture. It appears certain, indeed, that White American theological culture is integral and indispensable to the overall process of colonization and oppression under which Black people have suffered for many centuries.

Even though it is true that neither Black nor White is intrinsically good or evil, the fact remains that the phenomenon (form, figure, image, symbol) of a White Christ has had an enormous influence on the world. The observable, measurable image of a European Messiah is one of the most potent instruments of Euro-American imperialism by virtue of its especially demeaning psychological impact on peoples of African descent!

Therefore, the authors of *Your God Is Too White* conclude:

"Any person who hates himself has, in a very real sense, disqualified himself for an experience with God. Black Power seeks to destroy the negative self-concept and images (created in the white world and furthered by its institutions) that make black people hate themselves and view themselves as less than human. These negative concepts are replaced with a positive self-image which affirms the full humanity of blacks, the beauty of blackness, the rich legacy of black achievements and the potential of blacks for controlling their own destiny."[44]

The Challenge of Changing the Image

Dr. Roderick W. Pugh offers a psychological perspective on the changing relationships between Blacks and Whites which is worth considering here:

"Whites in this country have related to Blacks from a role concept of assumed superiority. Adaptive inferiority in Blacks not only is seen to be reactive to assumed superiority in Whites, but also it has served to support and perpetuate it. In other words, the self-concept of Whites to some degree has been organized around how they have seen themselves in relation to Blacks.

"It is hypothesized, therefore, that the basic process of the Black Revolution consists in fact of two self-concepts' effects: (a) there is a reintegration of self-concept on the part of Blacks, which entails the assumption of a positive sense of self-esteem and a rejection of adaptive inferiority; and (b) there is a forced reorganization of self-concept on the part of Whites, which undermines their assumed superiority to Blacks.

"This forced reorganization of self-concept, which negates the assumed superiority of Whites, is very threatening and anxiety-provoking to many Whites and results in various kinds of 'backlash' and in resistance against change."[45]

If Pugh is correct, these changes in self-perception in Blacks and Whites represent a transitional stage in race relations, the challenge and magnitude of which may lead to a genuine revolutionary movement in America.

In a sense, self-perception helps determine not only how we

view change, but also how we view ourselves.

"The individual's conception of himself is based on his perception of the way others are responding to him,"[46] says John W. Kinch in "Experiments on Factors Related to Self-Concept Change." According to Kinch, human interaction takes place with the aid of various forms of indirect communication such as signs, gestures, and language. Encounters with individuals are through outward symbols of recognition representing inward responses.

For example, language has multiple levels of meaning, both in what is said and what is meant, and may be variously interpreted according to one's personal understanding. Two communicators using the same language may have dissimilar meanings. Therefore, it is not only the symbolic responses but also the way those responses are perceived or interpreted which impacts on self-concept. Kinch further observes:

"The more important the individual perceives the contact between himself and the others to be, the more likely it is that the individual's perceptions of the responses of the others will be used in defining his self-image. It is widely accepted that contacts with 'significant others' are required before the individual's self-concept will be affected. These 'significant others' may take the form of prestigeful persons (experts) or of personal acquaintances (friends)."[47]

So we can see that the symbolic role of Jesus Christ as a "significant other," especially among Christians, is crucial in defining individual self-image. As a central theme of the Christian gospel, He may also be considered as a "language event"; that is, the Logos, the Interpretation, the Word of God. As such, He is the supreme symbol through whom God's responses to humanity are communicated, perceived, and used in defining individual self-images.

When Jesus Christ is viewed as the "significant other," the most important symbolic percept between interacting human parties, His effect on their self-images is mutually vital. Whether or not He is pictured as a Black African or White European ultimately may determine the kind of effect produced. It is logical that White images of Christ will be perceived by Blacks as a negative response from the White world, if not from God Himself.

The image of a White Messiah may be taken as an implicit

message that Whites are superior to Blacks. In consequence, Blacks may assume that their role and status are lower and less significant than the role and status of Whites. The conspicuous absence of Blackness in White images of Christ may be taken to mean Blacks are excluded from divine concern and esteem, that they are unworthy to be counted equal to Whites, and are incompatible with the pure and lofty ideals, values, and standards of Christianity.

Even worse, they may perceive themselves as deserving ill repute and abuse based on their extreme divergence from the supreme white norm. On the other hand, if the "significant other" would be portrayed more like themselves in color and/or features, their perception of society might have opposite, positive psychological effects.

These notions about the shape and meaning of Jesus change, depending on the view of the beholder. But as these notions about Jesus change, does Jesus change, too? No. They merely show that how Jesus is presented can change over time and space. The solution to this problem is before us. Indeed, the real test of the ultimate social impact of the Black Christ is the challenge of institutionalization.

That is to say, if Jesus is to be fully accepted as the Black Messiah who exists to liberate Black people from oppression—social, economic, political or psychological—this image and concept must be internalized in the Black community. To do this, the institutions of the Black home, school, and especially the church must begin to establish religious and theological traditions with the Black Messiah at the center. As the Association of Black Psychologists determined in 1980:

RESOLUTION
APPROVED AT THE 1980 ANNUAL MEETING
OF THE ASSOCIATION OF BLACK PSYCHOLOGISTS

WHEREAS: The portrayal of the Divine in images of Caucasian flesh constitutes an oppressive instrument destructive to the self-esteem of Black people throughout the world and is directly destructive to the psychological well-being of Black Children;

WHEREAS: The Association of Black Psychologists has condemned the negative portrayal of Blacks in media presentations in the past, we recognize the portrayal of the Divine as Caucasian as the most pervasive assertion of white supremacy. We see such grandiosity on the part of Caucasian people as destructive to themselves and damaging to people who accept white supremacy images as subliminal elements of their religious beliefs;

WHEREAS: There is a negative psychological impact when images of the Divinity and Divine figures are portrayed in Caucasoid flesh with Caucasoid features, the Association of Black Psychologists considers such portrayal as being a mechanism which insidiously advocates white supremacy and by implication Black inferiority.

WHEREAS: The Association of Black Psychologists, as practicing experts in human mental functioning, recognizes that the persistent exposure to such images is particularly damaging to immature Black minds;

RESOLVED: That the Association of Black Psychologists recommends the removal of Caucasoid images of the Divinity from public display and from places of worship, particularly in settings where immature Black minds are likely to be exposed.

RESOLVED: That the Association of Black Psychologists provide copies of this resolution to national religious bodies, national civil rights organizations, and to select religious leaders for the purpose of opening up an educational dialogue for change.[48]

The practical side of this issue of change has yet to amass the degree of support that its importance warrants. The following excerpt, taken from an article published in the *Los Angeles Sentinel*, the city's largest Black-owned paper, is titled "Children's Literature Designed for Blacks." It reports a meager scratching at the surface of the need:

"A new Sunday School literature designed to correct the impression that Jesus is white Anglo-Saxon or that Christianity is the white man's religion has been introduced by Urban Ministries, Inc. (UMI), the first predominantly black-owned independent publisher of religious curriculum literature. Called 'Primary Street' and planned especially for children ages 6–8, the literature depicts, more than most literature has done heretofore, Bible characters with the likeness of Middle Eastern and North African peoples."[49]

In an essay entitled "The Religion of Black Power," Vincent Harding anticipates the objection that graphic portrayals of God as Black may result in counter-distortions: "...Even if He is Black, the final glory is not the glory of blackness, but a setting straight of all the broken men and communities of the earth."[50]

The call goes out to hundreds of Black artists and writers to create new imagery, to create new imagery, to create new imagery.

One picture can be worth ten thousand words to the literate as well as the illiterate and the semi-literate. The latter are more dependent than the former on visual communication; what they come to believe about Jesus of Nazareth will be determined by what they see. Christ came as the visible Word, the Logos, the expression of the invisible God: He could be heard but He could be seen and touched too—if not with the hands—with the eyes, even from a distance.

In *Icon and Idea: The function of Art in the Development of Human Consciousness*, Herbert Read heavily underscores the crucial nature of symbolic imagery:

"It is only in so far as the artist establishes symbols for the representation of reality that mind, as a structure of thought, can take shape. The artist establishes these symbols by becoming conscious of new aspects of reality, and by representing his consciousness of these new aspects of reality in plastic or poetic images."[51]

If icon is the basis of idea then symbolism is the basis of reality. In practical terms this means the character of Black Theology must become more graphic in the future than it has been in the past. By "becoming conscious of new aspects of reality," the Black religious experience may yield a larger crop of symbolic representations as its necessary theological corollary.

If pictures are a "kind of visual preaching," then artists may accept their vocation as a calling from God when they are inspired to use their talents in the services of the religion or the Church. They should consider themselves as preachers of the Word: they should adorn the gospel with windows of vision in which human faith and divine grace can meet in mutual rapture. But they should also allow Canon Theodore O. Wedel's warning to ring loudly in the corridors of their memory: "Protestant churches, however, may be ready to open their doors again to ministry of color, as they have already admitted organ and song. They will need guidance."[52]

Explicitly, Jesus is the human incarnation of God; implicitly, He is God. He is the denotation and connotation of Deity. As such, He is the Alpha and Omega in the sacred symbolism of the

Christian church, Black and White. Therefore, any usage of symbolic imagery of Christ which is motivated by selfishness, as opposed to self-love, distorts the purpose for which He came, which is to represent God and not just humanity.

Footnotes

1. Eulalio P. Baltazar, *The Dark Center: A Process Theology of Blackness* (New York: Paulist Press, 1973), p. 32.
2. E. Franklin Frazier, *Negro Youth at the Crossroads: Their Personality Development in the Middle States* (New York: Schocken Books, 1940), p v.
3. F. Graeme Chalmers, "Art, Religion, and Education," *Religious Education* (July-August 1972), p. 284.
4. Rollo May, "The Significance of Symbols," *Symbolism in Religion and Literature*, ed., Rollo May (New York: George Braziller, Inc., 1958, 1960), p. 22.
5. Edith Kramer, *Art as Therapy with Children* (New York: Schocken Books, 1971), p. xiii.
6. Ibid., p. 149.
7. Eldridge Cleaver, *Soul on Ice* (New York: Dell Publishing Company, Inc., 1968), p. 161.
8. Franz Fanon, *Black Skin, White Masks* (New York: Grove Press, Inc., 1952, 1967), p. 160.
9. Alvin Poussaint, "The Negro American: His Self-Image and Integration," *The Black Power Revolt*, ed., Floyd B. Barbour (Boston: Porter Sargent Publisher, 1968), p. 96.
10. Ibid., p. 97.
11. Bracey, Meier and Rudwick, *Black Nationalism*, etc., p. 155.
12. Edward W. Blyden, *Christianity, Islam and the Negro Race* (Edinburgh: Edinburgh University Press, 1967, 1969), p. 353.
13. Warner R. Traynham, *Christian Faith in Black and White: A Primer in Theology from the Black Perspective* (Wakefield: The Parameter Press, Inc., 1973), p. 60.
14. Ibid.
15. Langdon Gilkey, *Naming the Whirlwind: The Renewal of God Language* (New York: The Bobbs-Merrill Company, Inc., 1969), p. 378.
16. Eric Kahler , "The Nature of the Symbol," *Symbolism in Religion and Literature*, ed., Rollo May (New York: George Braziller, Inc., 1958, 1960), p. 70.
17. F. W. Dillistone, "The Function of Symbols in Religious

Experience," *Myth and Symbol*, ed., F. W. Dillistone (London: Society for Promoting Christian Knowledge, 1966), p. 84.

18. Abraham Joshua Heschel, "Symbolism and the Jewish Faith," *Religious Symbolism*, ed., Ernest F. Johnson (Port Washington: Kennikat Press, Inc., 1955, 1969), p. 59.

19. Malachi Martin, *Jesus Now* (New York: E. P. Dutton and Company, Inc., Popular Library Edition, 1973), p. 12.

20. Na'im Akbar, *Chains and Images of Psychological Slavery* (Jersey City: New Mind Productions, 1984), p. 47.

21. Ibid., p. 66.

22. Rosemary Ruether, *Liberation Theology: Human Hope Confronts Christian History and American Power* (New York: Paulist Press, 1972), p. 128.

23. James M. Banks, "Racial Prejudice and the Black Self-Concept," *Black Self-Concept: Implications for Education and Social Change*, eds., James A. Banks and Jean D. Grambs (New York: McGraw-Hill Book Company), p. 8.

24. Cynthia N. Separd, "The World through Mark's Eyes," *Black Self Concept*, Ibid, p. 2.

25. S. Anita Stauffer, "Identification Theory and Christian Moral Education," *Religious Education* (Jan-Feb 1972), p. 61.

26. Gerardus van der Leeuw, *Sacred and Profane Beauty: the Holy in Art*.

27. Ibid.

28. Martin Luther King, Jr., *Where Do We Go From Here: Chaos or Community?* (New York: Harper and Row Publishers, Inc., 1967, 1968), p. 34.

29. Albert B. Cleage, Jr., *The Black Messiah* (New York: Sheed and Ward, 1969).

30. James H. Cone, *Black Theology and Black Power* (New York: Seabury Press, 1969).

31. C. Eric Lincoln, *The Black Church Since Frazier* (New York: Schocken Books, 1974), p. 148.

32. Paul Tillich, "The Religious Symbol," *Religious Symbolism*, Ibid., p. 108.

33. Alex Poinsett, "The Quest for a Black Christ," *Ebony* (March 1969), p. 174.

34. James H. Cone, *A Black Theology of Liberation* (New York: J. B. Lippincott Company, 1970), p. 114.

35. Ibid., p. 197.

36. Ammi, p. 21.

37. James H. Cone, *God of the Oppressed* (New York: Seabury Press, 1975), p. 136.

38. Ibid., pp. 108-137.

39. Cone, *A Black Theology of Liberation*, p. 69.

40. James H. Cone, *The Spirituals and the Blues* (New York: Seabury Press, 1972), p. 54.

41. Cone, *Black Theology and Black Power*, p. 69.

42. Ruether, p. 129.

43. Ibid., p. 133.

44. Columbus Salley and Roland Behm, *Your God is Too White* (Downers Grove: Inter-Varsity Press, 1970), p. 80.

45. Roderick W. Pugh, "Psychological Aspects of the Black Revolution," *Black Psychology*, ed., Reginald L. Jones (New York: Harper and Row Publishers, Inc., 1972), pp. 354-5.

46. John W. Kinch, "Experiments on Factors Related to Self-Concept Change," *Symbolic Interaction: A Reader in Social Psychology*, 2nd Ed., eds., Jerome G. Manis and Bernard Meltzer (Boston: Allyn and Bacon, Inc., 1967, 1972), p. 262.

47. Ibid., p. 263.

48. Akbar, appendix.

49. "Children's Literature Designed for Blacks," *Los Angeles Sentinel* (Thursday, Dec. 11, 1975), p. C-9.

50. Vincent Harding, "The Religion of Black Power," *Religious Situation*, ed., Donald R. Cutler (Boston: Beacon Press, 1968), p. 37.

51. Herbert Read, *Icon and Idea: The Function of Art in the Development of Human Consciousness* (New York: Schocken Books, 1972), p. 53.

52. Theodore A. Wedel, "Liturgy and Art," *Religion in Life* (Summer 1969), p. 209.

Come to me, all that labor and I will give you rest.

Chapter 5

Jesus the Liberator

From Luke 4:16-19: "Then Jesus went to Nazareth, and was handed the book of the prophet Isaiah. He unrolled the scroll and found the place where it is written,

"The spirit of the Lord is upon me, because he has chosen me to bring good news to the poor. He has sent me to proclaim liberty to the captives and recovery of sight to the blind, to set free the oppressed and announce that the time has come when the Lord will save his people."

From Isaiah 43:1-5: "Do not be afraid—I will save you. I have called you by name—you are mine. When you pass through deep waters, I will be with you, your troubles will not overwhelm you. When you pass through fire, you will not be burned, the hard trials that come will not hurt you. For I am the Lord your God, the holy God, the holy God of Israel, who saves you. I will give up Egypt to set you free; I will give up Sudan and Seba. I will give up whole nations to save your life, because you are precious to me and because I love you and give you honor. Do not be afraid—I am with you!"

In *Soul of the Black Preacher*, Joseph Johnson is unequivocal in his endorsement of "Jesus, the Liberator":

"The white Christ of the white church establishment is the enemy of the black man. The teachings of this white Christ are used to justify wars, exploitation, segregation, discrimination, prejudice, and racism. This white Christ is the oppressor of the black man and the black preacher and scholar were compelled to discover a Christ in his image of blackness. He was forced to look

59

at the teachings of Jesus in the light of his own black experience and discover what this black Jesus said about the realities of his own life."[1]

While the Black Messiah was not dumb and voiceless during centuries of unjust treatment of Blacks, Johnson complains of White deafness and indifference. He introduces the notion that the Black messianic voice of Jesus was not being heard because it spoke in southern plantation dialect and northern ghetto idioms. Traditional Afro-American language patterns were always considered inferior to Euro-American, Anglo-Saxon speech. The meaning of this ethnocentric mistake is that White Americans, and theologians established sound barriers around the Savior's Black preachers, missionaries, and evangelists.

If the Christian evangel is God's message to all people, then it is God's message to Black people. But how effective is a preached message that cannot be understood by those who hear it? Black Americans, like all other people, have a unique tongue; they have a special kind of communication skill wrought within their own specific culture. Therefore, the gospel of Christ translated into Black language is the only language that the Black masses can fully comprehend. When Black people hear God's message preached in their own tongue, then, and only then, are they assured of the reality of Jesus, the Black Liberator.

Gayraud Wilmore contends: "In the midst of suffering and conflict, the wretched of the earth, typified in Black Theology by the humiliated and exploited people of color, experience liberation by the power of God's saving word.

"To speak of Christ as the Black Messiah is rather to invest blackness...with religious meaning expressing the preeminent reality of black suffering,"[2] a suffering connected with the vicarious death of Jesus on the Cross. According to Wilmore, the death and resurrection of Jesus was "a liberating event," with radical, historical ramifications for the oppressed and their oppressors.

In sum, the issues joined in this debate revolve around the question of whether or not orthodox Christian theism has the actual "...capacity to exterminate oppression. ...."[3]

In any case, by investing Blackness with "symbolic meaning" related to "redemptive suffering," Wilmore shows how easy it is to identify the historical experience of Black suffering with messianic prophecy. He cites the suffering servant passage in Isaiah to illuminate this identification:

"He had no form or comeliness that we should look at him, and no beauty that we should desire him. He was despised and rejected by men; a man of sorrows, and acquainted with grief... And we esteemed him not."[4]

And further,

"He was oppressed, and he was afflicted, yet he opened not his mouth; like a lamb that is led to the slaughter, and like a sheep that before its shearers is dumb, so he opened not his mouth. By oppression and judgment he was taken away; and as for his generation, who considered that he was cut out of the land of the living." (Isaiah 53:1-3, 7-8)[5] Examined in this way, the Messiah is unmistakably identifiable with the Black experience in America.

The search for the Black Messiah is nothing less than a unique, ethnic consciousness in search of its own God and its own identity. "Basic to our struggle and the revitalization of the Black Church," says Cleage, "is the simple fact that we are building a totally new self-image. Our rediscovery of the Black Messiah is a part of our rediscovery of ourselves."[6]

J. Deotis Roberts views the Black Messiah as a symbol and as a myth, both of which point beyond themselves to what they participated in as well as represent. As myth the Black Messiah is the expression of both literal and imagined reality as they coexist in Black consciousness. Myth places human encounters with life forces into a pattern that reflects a personal or cultural world view. For instance, a mythical personage may be a real or ideal hero whose experiences represent the collective life involvements of a given group of people.[7]

Oppression and suffering among Black masses in the Diaspora is an example of "encounters with life forces" which form a common bond. The myth that Blacks are docile, submissive, patient, and passive is one way they have been stereotypically identified. In an article entitled "Black Power in Christological Perspective," Professor William H. Becker suggests that a composite picture of Jesus Christ be considered as the most appropriate model.

"Perhaps the appropriate model of manhood for the black American in this moment is Christ the rebel, informed by Christ the sufferer, and for the white American, Christ the sufferer, with an understanding that Christ was a rebel too."[8]

Becker proposes a correction to the weak, Uncle Tom image of

Christ by emphasizing the strong, aggressive, rebellious nature of suffering.

Similarly, suffering as a form of rebelling, resisting and fighting back was articulated in the following statement by Dr. Martin Luther King, Jr.:

"To our most bitter opponents we say: 'We shall match your capacity to inflict suffering by our capacity to endure suffering. We shall meet your physical force with soul force. Do to us what you will, and we shall continue to love you...Beat us and leave us half dead, and we shall still love you. But be ye assured that we will wear you down by our capacity to suffer.' "[9]

Whatever else may be said of King's philosophy of nonviolence, the suffering he advocated was certainly motivated by a spirit of rebellion against injustice and oppression. The redemptive suffering of Jesus as the Black Messiah must likewise be seen in the light of His work of rebellion, "...for if Jesus was a sufferer, he was also a rebel, a rebel with a cause who suffered for that cause."[10] As a corrective to stereotypical portrayals of Black suffering, acknowledgement of its rebellious character is a welcome gesture.

Dr. King's career as a social activist and a civil rights and anti-war leader may have obscured his role as a profound theological thinker and philosopher. Like so many members of the Black intelligentsia before him, King was thrust into the streets as an advocate of racial justice and equality. As an idealist and an integrationist, his philosophy did not permit him to focus exclusively on the needs of his own ethnic group. There are those who contend that he was a theologian who was Black but that he was not a Black theologian. The glue binding King to "the American dream" came from his application of the Judeo-Christian ethic to the "American dilemma." Therefore, perhaps it would be incorrect to assume that he fully grasped the extent of the alienation that existed between Blacks and Whites.

But King as an "exemplary model" of Black manhood commanded such respect and admiration that he was thought of as being "like Jesus" in some circles. Hence, many younger and older Blacks learned to take pride in themselves and their people through King's example. This example, it should be noted, is intricately bound to the supreme model of Jesus, the Liberator.

Footnotes

1. Joseph A. Johnson, Jr., *The Soul of the Black Preacher* (Philadelphia: United Church Press, 1971), p. 90.
2. Gayraud S. Wilmore, "The Black Messiah: Revising the Color Symbolism of Western Christology," *Journal of the Inter-Denominational Theological Center*, Vol. 2 (Fall 1974), p. 18, 13-4.
3. William R. Jones, *Is God a White Racist?: A Preamble to Black Theology* (Garden City: Doubleday and Company, Inc., 1973), p. 147.
4. Wilmore, p. 13.
5. Ibid.
6. Cleage, p. 7.
7. J. Deotis Roberts, *Liberation and Reconciliation: A Black Theology* (Philadelphia: Westminister Press, 1971), pp. 132-4.
8. William H. Becker, "Black Power in Christological Perspective," *Religion in Life*, Vol. XXXVIII, No. 3 (Autumn 1969), p. 414.
9. Ibid., p. 407.
10. Ibid., p. 411.

Epilogue

One of the objectives of this book was to refute the image of Jesus Christ as being White. This we believe was demonstrated with biblical references, Christ's family lineage on Earth, the geographical location of His birth and time on Earth, and with artistic representations of Jesus before and after the commissioning of Michelangelo. Another parallel objective was to extract and formulate the Black image of Jesus Christ from the above sources. And, although it should be noted that these sources represent circumstantial evidence—as they must, since there was no photograph taken of Christ—nonetheless the evidence stands as an undeniable response to the question, "What color was Jesus?": Jesus Christ was a Black man.

The psychological significance of this evidential response is based on an unfortunate reality. Having been indoctrinated with a White image of Christ and then experiencing that image's sudden removal—via the presentation of such strong evidence as has been given here—does not eliminate the notion of a White Christ from among the beliefs held by many Blacks. What must first occur is a transitional period.

For some Blacks, the transitional route may encompass that of moving spiritually and mentally from a White image of Jesus to no distinct, racial image. This of course is difficult to achieve without an alternative, concrete form to take its place. For others, the more natural path toward change involves the acceptance of the Black Christ.

The impact of a White image of Jesus has been devastating on the Black community. It has reduced the number of Black men who worship and the self-determination of the remaining congregation to believe they have control over their lives. This racist image of a White Christ resulted from a lack of appreciation for the distinct differences between peoples and a need to rationalize a people's supposed superiority. Eventually, it is hoped that all people will feel secure enough to be comfortable with each other's differences, and will encourage everyone to define for themselves what are correct, good and bad, images of beauty and their God who has chosen all of creation within which to manifest His greatness.

In the meantime, the ideal—that every race of people has the right to portray God in their own image, and that no race should determine another's image of God—has yet to be reached.

Obviously, a people that will allow others to determine the image of God to be portrayed, will allow others to control other images, goods and services, and every other necessity of life.

The ultimate objective goes beyond this book. *What Color was Jesus?* was an attempt to correct a wrong and to provide a self-esteeming, affirmative image for Black people. The ultimate objective would not be to major in minors and make the color of Jesus more important than who Jesus was, what He stood for, and how we can emulate Him.

INDEX